Praise for

VALUE CREATION INSIGHTS

"Bartley Madden's book provides a compelling and powerful account of a systems approach to business. It demonstrates how shareholder value is derivative of a purpose of business that places knowledge creation at its core. The book draws on the immense amount of practical experience as well as academic knowledge that Bartley brings to the subject. It deserves to be widely read and highly influential on business thinking and practice."

Colin Mayer CBE
Professor Emeritus, University of Oxford

"Madden's systems perspective provides a great framework for corporations to leverage their Balanced Scorecard for rapid strategy adaptation in a fast-changing world. The ideas in *Value Creation Insights* enable a firm to embed the key variables for long-term value creation within the causal linkages of its strategy map and scorecard. The pragmatic theory's emphasis on knowledge-building proficiency shows that long-term, sustainable performance starts by motivating and enhancing specific capabilities of those closest to the firm's value-creating work."

Robert S. Kaplan
Professor Emeritus, Harvard Business School; coauthor,
The Balanced Scorecard: Translating Strategy into Action

"I have been waiting for a book that successfully translates the insights of systems thinking into a theory of the firm. Bartley Madden's book outlining his Pragmatic Theory of the Firm successfully achieves this. Starting with the idea that a firm is a holistic system seeking to create value, the book is suffused with systems ideas. It argues that firms should serve a fourfold purpose, emphasizes knowledge building, foregrounds interrelationships, and challenges command-and-control thinking. It advocates taking multiple perspectives to encourage constructive skepticism. The book is a provocation to systems thinkers to contribute to the further development of Bart Madden's Pragmatic Theory of the Firm."

Michael C. Jackson OBE
Professor Emeritus, University of Hull

"On first impression, Bartley Madden's book, *Value Creation Insights*, appears to be yet another book about how companies can create value. But it's actually something much simpler, yet more profound: A series of insights by a shrewd analyst, gained over a half a century of examining what works, what doesn't, and why. Madden's system-based analysis makes you wish you had read this book earlier in your career, no matter where in your career you are now."

Jon Lukomnik
Managing Partner, Sinclair Capital; coauthor, *Adapt or Fail!:
A 5x5 Governance Framework for Boards of Directors*

"Bartley Madden's latest book encapsulates a lifetime of insights gleaned from a successful career providing investment research to money managers. Madden challenges traditional thinking in accounting and finance by questioning the usefulness of the underlying economic theory of the firm in these two disciplines. Based on narrow self-interest and conflicts of interest between principals and agents throughout the firm, agency theory focuses on controlling activities and opportunistic behavior in order to control costs. Madden convincingly argues that agency theory is unable to capture value creation in the modern economy driven by innovation, rapidly evolving technologies, and intangible assets. He presents a new Pragmatic Theory of the Firm based on knowledge building and valuation creation being inextricably linked. The chapter on the New Economy Accounting is based on a paper he and I coauthored that presents a workable plan to finally integrate intangible assets into our accounting system. The pragmatic result would be more accurate accounting return metrics for a firm's business units and improved resource allocation decisions."

Douglas E. Stevens
Professor and Copeland/Deloitte Chair of Accountancy,
Robinson College of Business, Georgia State University

"Investment theories to date have largely been mathematical propositions, connecting risk and return quantitatively. What have been missing are verbal propositions that logically and intuitively connect investment returns to the drivers of those returns. Bartley Madden's new book offers such a tangible proposition with his Pragmatic Theory of the Firm. The theory proposes a four-dimensional firm purpose, whereby maximizing shareholder value is best positioned not as the purpose of the firm but as the result of a firm successfully achieving its purpose. This integrated framework is indeed pragmatically logical and intuitive. Even better, its insights and action implications are equally powerful for academics and students, for corporate board members and executives, and for institutional investors and their clients."

Keith Ambachtsheer
Executive-in-Residence, Rotman School of Management, University of Toronto; Director Emeritus, International Centre for Pension Management; author of four books on pension design, governance, and investing; advisor to major pension funds around the world

"Madden brings forward essential guidance on how organizations can thrive for the long term, bringing value to those who depend on them and creating sustainable entities that innovate over many lifetimes. I often cite Madden's work in my presentations and writing because his ideas change people's perspectives for the better. His redefinition of 'firm risk' is critical, especially as he integrates it with his Life-Cycle of the Firm and the Knowledge-Building Loop. You and any organization you serve will be better off by reading and adopting Bart's ideas."

David R. Koenig
Author, *Governance Reimagined: Organizational Design, Risk, and Value Creation, The Board Member's Guide to Risk,* and *Life at the Nexus: Understanding Ourselves and the Power of Interconnectedness*

"Bartley Madden's Pragmatic Theory of the Firm uniquely combines knowledge building and value creation to deliver a theoretically sound and practical theory of the firm that deserves to be taught in business schools. I highly recommend this book to my students, alumni, fellow faculty members, and to the business leaders and entrepreneurs I advise. Over many years, Madden has presented key ideas in *Value Creation Insights* to my MBA students that complemented my teaching. This joint effort helped students integrate traditional siloed business courses, which include finance, accounting, economics, strategy, marketing, production processes, leadership/ethics/corporate governance, and business history."

Dr. Mark L. Frigo
Distinguished Professor Emeritus, Director of the Center for Strategy, Execution, and Valuation, Kellstadt Graduate School of Business, DePaul University; coauthor with Joel Litman, *DRIVEN: Business Strategy, Human Actions, and the Creation of Wealth*

"Bartley Madden's Pragmatic Theory of the Firm is aligned with how we believe great companies are built. As long-term active investors, we are committed to understanding how companies focus on these critical attributes of culture and innovation regardless of how difficult they can be to measure. We believe deep research and analysis of how a company operates and is managed provides long-term investors unique economic opportunities because they aren't always obvious to see. We also are encouraged by Bartley's ability to articulate 'what it takes' to be a great company. It is an excellent piece of work that helps demonstrate why we do the homework to identify these core principles and how we think about creating long-term value in client portfolios. The investment world has become so short-term and has unappreciated the importance of accountability to stewardship. This book helps bring it to life, and we applaud Bartley for making it so clear!"

Carol W. Geremia
President, Co-Head of Global Distribution, MFS Investments

amplify

an imprint of Amplify Publishing Group

www.amplifypublishinggroup.com

Value Creation Insights: A Foundational Understanding of How Firms Build Knowledge and Create Value

For more information, please contact:
Amplify Publishing, an imprint of Amplify Publishing Group
620 Herndon Parkway, Suite 220
Herndon, VA 20170
info@amplifypublishing.com

Library of Congress Control Number: 2025911604

CPSIA Code: PRV0825A

ISBN-13: 979-8-89138-653-2

Printed in the United States

In celebration of my family—

Maricela, Lucinda, Miranda, Jeffrey, Gregory, Peg, Katie, and Sarah

VALUE CREATION INSIGHTS

A FOUNDATIONAL UNDERSTANDING OF HOW FIRMS **BUILD KNOWLEDGE** AND **CREATE VALUE**

BARTLEY J. MADDEN

amplify
an imprint of Amplify Publishing Group

CONTENTS

Foreword

In today's incredibly dynamic business world, where rapid change and uncertainty often shape our daily decisions, there is an urgent need for a clear framework to guide value creation and long-term success. This book is a culmination of decades of Bart Madden's research, practical experience, and deep thinking, in a career spanning engineering, military service, business innovation, and investment research.

The book is grounded in the critical idea that knowledge-building and value creation are inextricably linked. By embracing systems thinking, Madden invites us to view firms as complex, holistic systems where each part plays a vital role in achieving long-term success. This book is not merely a set of theories—it is a framework for understanding how businesses can evolve, adapt, and thrive in an increasingly interconnected and dynamic world. Madden's Knowledge-Building Loop is a tangible process for improving creativity, problem-solving, and strategic decision-making. He connects these concepts to real-world examples, from the Wright brothers to Amazon and John Deere.

Bart Madden is a lifelong advocate for the creation of lasting value, where his thinking is advanced through the Madden Center for Value Creation at Florida Atlantic University. Our center seeks to foster a deeper understanding of what drives value within firms and to explore the critical intersections between knowledge, culture, systems thinking, and financial performance. The principles shared in this book offer a roadmap for how to build the types of systems, cultures, and mindsets that can lead to superior value creation—exactly the kind of knowledge the Madden Center aims to impart to its students and the broader business community.

This is not a book meant solely for academics or theorists. Its insights are designed for practitioners at every level of business—from managers and directors to entrepreneurs and students—offering tools and perspectives that are directly applicable to their roles. Through his clear and accessible writing style, supported by numerous figures and footnotes for those wishing to dive deeper, Madden makes complex concepts comprehensible and actionable.

As you read through this book, you will not only gain a richer understanding of what drives business success, but also find yourself challenged to rethink how you approach problems, innovation, and growth. This book invites intellectual curiosity, promotes systems thinking, and empowers its readers to create lasting value in a world that increasingly demands thoughtful, informed leadership.

I am confident that this book will become a valuable resource for all who seek to understand the deeper mechanisms behind value creation.

Enjoy the journey of learning and discovery that lies ahead.

Siri Terjesen
Associate Dean, Phil Smith Professor of Entrepreneurship,
and Executive Director of the Madden Center for Value Creation
at the Florida Atlantic University College of Business

Preface and Overview

This book is intended for managers, boards of directors, investors, students and teachers in business/finance/economics courses, employees with an eye on promotion and increased responsibilities, and, in general, anyone who is intellectually curious about how firms outperform and underperform in creating long-term value. This book will go a long way in helping us to understand the proper role of business in a thriving capitalist economy and why the firm is the most important entity in a capitalist economy.

By way of background, during the 1960s, I began my career as an engineer then subsequently spent time in the army during the Vietnam War. In seeking a career change that I could be passionate about, I attended the University of California, Berkeley business school. I then cofounded Callard, Madden & Associates, an investment research firm. This led to developing two research questions that have guided my lifelong educational journey: What causes firms over their life cycle to create more/less value than the average firm? How best to connect a firm's long-term financial performance to its market valuation? My answer to these questions is encapsulated in the Pragmatic Theory of the Firm discussed in chapter 1.

Writing this book at the youthful age of eighty-one, I feel extraordinarily fortunate that my energy for work has remained at a high level and that I have been able to sail where the wind blew on my educational journey. Case in point: My research on value creation led to systems thinking becoming the north star for my work and the thread that connects the chapters in this book.

Another case in point: After decades of studying the histories of firms, I concluded that a knowledge-building culture is the critical determinant of long-term performance. This has led to an ongoing project to better understand how we build knowledge. The Knowledge-Building Loop (analyzed in chapter 2) has proven especially useful in my work and in helping others understand the holistic nature of the firm.

Hopefully, after reading this book, you will find the Knowledge-Building Loop to be a practical means to improve your creativity, and that this book's six key insights, detailed below, deserve inclusion in your problem-solving/thinking toolbox.

Six Key Insights

- Knowledge building and value creation are opposite sides of the same coin. Deeper understanding of a customer's pain point in accomplishing a needed task, solving a technical problem to more efficiently manufacture a product, and other knowledge improvements are prerequisites to creating value.

- Systems thinking provides actionable insights by clarifying a system's goal, the interrelationships among the system's parts, and the critical constraints impeding the achievement of the system goal. Systems thinking can counterbalance our inclination to constrict the scope of problems to make them more manageable. Systems thinking is also the key to discovering faulty policies and obsolete assumptions high in the organization that show up as lower-level problems that are never resolved. Systems thinking complements constructive skepticism about what we think we know.

- The Pragmatic Theory of the Firm views the firm as a holistic system for creating value, thereby providing a more insightful understanding of a firm's history, its competitive advantage (if any), and its shareholder returns. Moreover, a deeper understanding of how a firm operates as a system sets the stage for exploring new value creation possibilities. Systems thinking and the Pragmatic Theory of the Firm are a hand-in-glove fit.

- Insights about the knowing process via the Knowledge-Building Loop help to better appreciate context, to see problems with alternative perspectives, and to ask better questions. This can lead to the big idea—discovering the critical obsolete assumption or customer understanding that once articulated becomes immediately useful because it explains so much.

- Language is perception's silent partner. Attention to language offers an actionable pathway to disentangle the assumptions behind the words that may in turn reveal the root cause of a problem or expose a strongly held but obsolete assumption.
- An individual's worldview is the automatic pilot for perceiving problems, choosing data to analyze, and developing solutions. Learning to experience alternative ways of seeing (a major benefit of systems thinking) can surmount this limitation and lead to a changed and improved worldview.

Chapter 1 notes the accelerating complexity due to today's interconnected challenges of technical, sociopolitical, and environmental issues, which in turn continually challenge firms to adapt and sustain value creation in a fast-changing world. Systems thinking is needed to manage this complexity. The uniquely successful Vanguard Method developed by John Seddon for service businesses is reviewed as an application of systems thinking firmly rooted in creating value for customers. The history of theories of the firm is briefly reviewed. The Pragmatic Theory of the Firm treats the firm as a holistic system and provides needed clarity as to the firm's purpose. Importantly, the pragmatic theory, in contrast to other theories of the firm, utilizes a life-cycle framework that links financial performance to the firm's market valuation and helps management and the board focus on the key issue(s) for value creation given the firm's life-cycle position. Historical analysis of firms invariably involves understanding the firm's culture. Social norms play a critical role in a firm's culture. The importance of culture is seen in the review of the life-cycle track records for Eastman Kodak and Intuit.

Chapter 2 explains the Knowledge-Building Loop in detail while showing how it connects to more well-known cognitive concepts. Creativity is discussed in the context of how the brain works. In a nutshell, creativity is a function of how rich in experiences one's brain memory bank is and the ability to retrieve relevant memories and make novel connections for the problem/project at hand. Our brains are hardwired to store experiences that potentially can be helpful in the future. It seems plausible that the Knowledge-Building Loop can upgrade storage and later retrieval of life experiences (including reading about business successes/failures) that may prove useful for future value creation opportunities. For example, a core reason for Amazon's success was CEO Jeff Bezos's worldview that enabled him to see opportunities unconstrained by Amazon's existing businesses. The Loop's components can help provide a means to categorize experiences to facilitate efficient retrieval. The Knowledge-Building Loop is used to analyze the fascinating details about the Wright brothers teaching the world how to fly. Finally, the ideas in this chapter shed light on academic criticisms of the Lean Startup methodology for entrepreneurs.

Chapter 3 discusses several different (yet similar) approaches to value creation/problem-solving. Imagination is this chapter's lead topic since it has been gaining momentum in business as a means to facilitate innovation. Imagination is central to design thinking that focuses on prototypes to gain rapid feedback similar to the Lean Startup. Next is an overview of the problem-solving approach used by the consulting firm McKinsey. Although lean thinking is typically considered as an approach to improving production efficiency, its scope is wider. Lean thinking is a different way of building capabilities that both shape and are shaped by strategy. Getting the value proposition right is critically important to successful innovation. In grappling with problems and creative solutions, a mental habit often obstructs (i.e., the names of things can restrict our ability to imagine alternative uses for them, which is called functional fixedness). Artificial intelligence (AI) can help circumvent this roadblock.

Chapter 4 discusses command-and-control hierarchical organizational structures versus flatter structures and the implications of the latter for sustaining a knowledge-building culture. An innovative European way to address this fundamental organizational issue eliminates budgets—the lifeblood of command-and-control hierarchies. Analyzing the organizational structure for megaprojects (skyscrapers, tunnels, etc.) provides applicable insights for business organization. Details are provided for the highly effective organizational structures of the preeminent steel manufacturer Nucor and the large global firm Haier Group. Also highlighted is the challenge facing Bayer AG management as it radically dismantles its command-and-control structure. This chapter ends by offering practical steps for a successful transition to a flatter organizational structure.

Chapter 5 overviews the early development of the life-cycle framework at Callard, Madden & Associates, which includes a valuation model and life-cycle track records. Systems thinking sets the stage for long-term improvement of this framework and a related global database that is now used worldwide by large money-management organizations for analyzing stock investments. The life-cycle framework is used to explain why Walmart outperformed the S&P 500 thirteenfold from 1980 to 1990 in a far more visually insightful manner than Excel spreadsheets.

Chapter 6 explains why our current accounting system is obsolete due to ignoring, in almost all cases, intangible assets—the key driver of competitive advantage in the New Economy. The result is significantly inaccurate accounting returns (e.g., return on net assets [RONA], return on invested capital [ROIC]). A solution is described that is both practical and not dependent upon the accounting rule makers.

Chapter 7 describes my Free to Choose Medicine proposal—a systems thinking approach that offers a competitive alternative to the US Food and Drug Administration's (FDA's) regulatory system. Specifically, patients, advised by their doctors, would be able to make informed decisions about early access to not-yet-approved drugs that have demonstrated initial safety and efficacy. At the start of the second Trump administration, I am optimistic that there will be legislation implementing structural change at the FDA consistent with Free to Choose Medicine principles.

Chapter 8 provides a visual summary of the key ideas in this book; describes new perspectives on value creation, value capture, and how competition works in multiple directions via networks; and recommends several enhancements to the Balanced Scorecard framework to facilitate practical experiences with critical value creation ideas. Finally, I offer my thoughts on why this book merits adoption in business schools.

The Appendix contains my commencement speech given at Florida Atlantic University's business school. The speech provides insights for how to use the ideas in this book for managing one's business career.

A final thought: I write to explain ideas with simple, direct language, stripped of academic jargon. However, at the same time, I believe it is essential to grasp key state-of-the-art ideas for the many topics covered; hence, in parts of the book, there are many endnotes for those wanting to dig deeper. Finally, the heavy use of figures is a result of me being a visual thinker in the extreme who equates understanding with drawing insightful pictures.

CHAPTER 1

A Theory of the Firm Needs Systems Thinking

In contemplating questions about the design, development, and delivery of systems, we need to draw on not just the life, physical, and social sciences in describing what a system does and how it does it, but also the humanities in considering why systems are created, why they exist, and what they do. Every part of our intellectual understanding and knowledge is therefore relevant to systems.[1]

—COLIN MAYER

This chapter first explains the importance of systems thinking as a way of seeing and gaining insights about firms. Next, the objectives of a theory of the firm in general are specified, illustrating their usefulness for practitioners and academics. This sets the stage for describing well-known theories of the firm while introducing the systems-based Pragmatic Theory of the Firm. Benefits from the latter include improved understanding and decision-making for managers, boards of directors, and investors.

Cause and Effect, Complexity, and Systems Thinking

The environmental, political, social, and economic challenges that we face are complex, to say the least, and require much more than reductionistic thinking. The complexity emerges from challenges that are not amenable solely to linear cause-and-effect analyses.

We experience life while solving (and avoiding) problems that block our intended objectives. Our knowledge base grows as we break apart problems and learn to associate cause and effect. This reductionistic approach consists of linear cause and effect (i.e., event A causes event B, and that, in turn, causes event C). This approach facilitates scientific experiments and has led to advancements in science.

A system is comprised of interdependent parts, with the whole having a specific purpose. While linear thinking connects events, systems thinking focuses on the interrelationships between the parts and the whole; the latter addresses how (e.g., feedback loops) and why events happen. Positive feedback adds to the momentum of the current direction, whereas negative feedback reduces the discrepancy between the actual versus the desired state. And time lags in feedback can add significant complexity to a system.[2] As a person's responsibilities increase in their work environment, the more critical becomes their need for skill in systems thinking.

Understanding and addressing today's problems should begin with constructive skepticism about how the problem is perceived and conceptualized. Constructive skepticism is part of the knowledge-building process, which will be addressed in chapter 2. A background in systems thinking facilitates an appreciation for the complexity of the system in which the problem is situated. Systems thinking is necessary for our modern, highly complex world but, unfortunately, is only slowly impacting the management of organizations. Michael C. Jackson, a leader in systems thinking, both practical and theoretical, tells us:

> What help can decision-makers expect when tackling the "messes" and "wicked problems" that proliferate in this age of complexity? They are usually brought up on classical management theory that emphasizes the need to forecast, plan, organize, lead, and control.

This approach relies on there being a predictable future environment in which it is possible to set goals that remain relevant into the foreseeable future; on enough stability to ensure that tasks arranged in a fixed hierarchy continue to deliver efficiency and effectiveness; on a passive and unified workforce; and on a capacity to take control action on the basis of clear measures of success. These assumptions do not hold in the modern world . . . [They] are simple, "quick-fix" solutions that flounder in the face of interconnectedness, volatility, and uncertainty. . . . In the absence of more thoroughly researched [systems thinking] ways forward, however, managers are left to persevere with their favorite panacea . . . or to turn to whatever new fad has hit the market.[3]

This brief explanation of systems thinking plus the discussion on the next page about the Vanguard Method is sufficient for the level of analysis used throughout this book. Here are some additional takeaways from leading systems thinkers suggesting that upgrading one's systems thinking capability offers a high return.

Russell Ackoff emphasized that a properly designed system does things right (efficiency) and creates value by doing the right things (effectiveness).[4] Consequently, clarity is needed to connect a system's purpose with performance metrics. Donella Meadows argued that there are no separate systems. Rather, the world is a continuum, and specifying a system's boundary depends upon the questions asked.[5] Jay Forrester explained that frequently a system's leverage points (targets for maximum performance gains) are counterintuitive.[6] His 1969 book, *Urban Dynamics,* was criticized because his systems analysis presciently demonstrated that subsidized low-income housing is a leverage point: and the less of it, then the better off *all* the city inhabitants. This contravened the national policy at that time. Systems thinking can, according to Michael Jackson, enable decision-makers and policymakers to improve imaginative capability and to tie in to powerful ways of thinking that transcend linear cause-and-effect methodology.[7]

The Vanguard Method

In the 1980s, John Seddon, while working as a prison psychologist, developed the (systems thinking) idea that changes in system design were far more effective than trying to help people individually. In the 1990s, Seddon honed the Vanguard Method for improving the performance of service organizations. He liberated management thinking that was typically blocked by conventional performance metrics. In 2003, he published *Freedom from Command and Control: A Better Way to Make the Work Work.* The book explains the foundational systems concepts that led to exceptional performance gains by his clients worldwide.

Seddon and his colleagues have a track record for demonstrating that the conventional management belief of a tradeoff between reducing costs or improving service is false. Moreover, the knowledge gained from systems thinking is transferred to both management and key operational employees, thereby enabling sustained superior performance. Implementing systems thinking that fundamentally changes how people think is an enormously powerful lever for improving overall system performance.

It is worthwhile to dig deeper into the Vanguard Method because the typical service organization does not have the complexities associated with manufacturing businesses. Consequently, the key systems ideas are easier to visualize and understand. The crux of the Vanguard Method is that management's strong beliefs (assumptions) shape how they perceive problems and how they orchestrate change to improve performance. However, most often management's assumptions are rooted in a command-and-control hierarchy—designed to control activities in order to control costs. Yet, often this control increases costs abetted by conventional accounting.

As to systems design, Seddon argues that service organization systems should be driven by what really matters (i.e., customer demand). In this way, employees doing the work can easily adapt to changes in customer demand. Performance metrics should provide information enabling those doing the work to improve their performance. The Vanguard Method separates customer demand into *value demand* and *failure demand,* the latter caused by failing to provide the desired customer experiences. Seddon emphasizes:

Managing with functional measures always causes suboptimization, because parts achieve their ends at the expense of the whole . . . Controlling work through functional measures can only be harmful to flow. All work goes through some kind of flow, so we would be better having measures of it.

Only by managing costs end-to-end, associating costs with flow, can you reduce costs in a sustainable manner. . . . In the current management philosophy, it is assumed that the bottom line can be influenced by using functional measures, targets, and standards to direct performance. . . . By their very nature, service demands contain high levels of variety. To tackle variety with command-and-control methods is to stifle the organization's ability to absorb it effectively. . . . The better able an organization is to absorb variety, the better the flow, hence the lower the costs and the better the service.[8]

Consider the management of an insurance claims provider that measures the number of calls taken per day by agents, the time spent on a call, and the total time to settle a claim and deliver a check. From a systems perspective, what is missing? Begin with the purpose: to deliver the desired customer experience of a speedy receipt of a fairly compensated check for damages incurred. The time to efficiently deliver that experience reflects value work. Time that exceeds that standard represents waste that should be communicated in an actionable format. Employees should receive performance information that identifies the sources of waste coupled to responsibility and the capability to take needed improvement actions. A properly designed system promotes a knowledge-building culture with a positive feedback loop to improve performance wherein performance shortfalls are identified and corrective actions follow.

Note the similarities between the Vanguard Method and lean thinking. The latter specifies a value stream (value-added steps) for each product plus horizontal flow that enables customers to pull value from the producer as opposed to pushing products to customers.

In summary, the Vanguard Method echoes one of the six key insights described earlier in the preface and overview: Knowledge building and value creation are opposite sides of the same coin.

The Need for a More Comprehensive Theory of the Firm

Theories shape your worldview, which, in turn, determines how you perceive the world, identify problems (opportunities), develop solutions (business plans), and even influence the data selected to test proposed ideas. Your worldview orchestrates feedback concerning your assumptions about how the world works that hopefully will improve your knowledge base. Everyone in business benefits from a useful theory of the firm. In addition, policymakers and even ordinary citizens benefit from understanding how the business firm is the engine of economic progress. Indeed, John Micklethwait and Adrian Wooldridge assert: "The most important organization in the world is the company: the basis of the prosperity of the West and the best hope for the future of the rest of the world."[9]

The importance of explicitly stating common sense objectives for a theory of the firm cannot be overstated. Absent these objectives, business school students are fed theories that seem plausible for a specific context—agency theory for corporate governance—but do not travel well in addressing all such objectives. The Pragmatic Theory of the Firm has four objectives not adequately addressed by any other theory. They are pragmatic because they are attuned to important decisions made by management, boards of directors, and investors:

- Facilitates systems thinking
- Provides clarity as to the purpose of the firm
- Identifies the critical determinant of the firm's long-term performance
- Connects the firm's long-term performance to market valuation and shareholder returns

These four objectives enable viewing the firm as a holistic system with connected activities—the bedrock of the pragmatic theory. In contrast, other theories of the firm can be categorized (as noted below) based on a single important issue that is of keen interest to the theory developers.

Since a strong case can be made that firms are the engine of economic progress, economists and other researchers who study progress invariably must explain the role of firms, hence the need for a theory. Attention to the theory developer's worldview explains the critical question they selected and how they answered it. The following overview briefly highlights notable theories (not a comprehensive review) in order to contrast them with the Pragmatic Theory of the Firm.

Neoclassical economics aggregates fundamental economic assumptions into a logically tight format. It integrates cost-of-production theory from classical economics with supply/demand and marginal cost analysis plus utility maximization. Neoclassical economists configure the firm as a black box that makes decisions ensuring marginal cost equals marginal revenue. Although this informs how an economic system attains equilibrium in stylized mathematical terms, it is nevertheless useless for understanding our four key objectives, and hence what is really going on in the black box.

Ronald Coase was awarded the Nobel Prize in economics partly for his 1937 article that explained why firms exist.[10] He saw the critical activity of the firm as providing a lower cost alternative to market transactions. So simple, yet so insightful. In his worldview:

> Economics has been becoming more and more abstract, less and less related to what goes on in the real world. In fact, economists have devoted themselves to studying imaginary systems, and they don't distinguish between the imaginary system and the real world. That's what modern economics has been and continues to be. All the prestige goes to people who produce the most abstract results about an economic system that doesn't exist.[11]

Coase opened the door for Oliver Williamson and others to develop the transactions cost theory of the firm that explains why firms choose different organizational forms.[12] This theory was then extended to control rights over the firm's assets.[13]

With his *Capitalism, Socialism, and Democracy* (1942), Joseph Schumpeter took a systems perspective and criticized neoclassical economics for downplaying the role of entrepreneurship. Edith Penrose's *Theory of the Growth of the Firm* (1959) focused on the utilization of the firm's resources to explain long-term growth. Jay Barney carried this line of thinking forward with the resource-based theory of the firm attuned to difficult-to-duplicate resources that can lead to competitive advantage.[14]

A better understanding of how firms utilize resources can provide insights about economic progress. Barney summarizes:

> And, what is personally satisfying is that resource-based theory really is a theory about inequality in society. While acknowledging that sometimes inequality in outcomes can be inefficient, even evil, resource-based theory's core message is: heterogeneity in outcomes in society is common and natural and is often good for all of us, those who are advantaged as well as those who are disadvantaged. If firms are "better off" because they are more skilled at addressing customer needs, then this inequality in outcomes is perfectly consistent with maximizing social welfare in society.[15]

A deeper understanding of firms must necessarily grapple with how management actually makes decisions and how knowledge is continually created. This was the goal of Richard Cyert and James March in their 1963 book, *A Behavioral Theory of the Firm*. Knowledge building is a logical fit with resources that can enable competitive advantage.

Robert Grant is a developer of the knowledge-based theory of the firm.[16] He informs us that:

> As competition intensifies and the pace of change accelerates across most business sectors, the coordination requirements for firms becomes increasingly complicated. Firms increasingly need

to simultaneously pursue multiple performance goals—cost, efficiency, quality, innovation, and flexibility. Explicit consideration of the knowledge management requirements of these complicated coordination patterns can offer us insight into the choice and design of organizational structures.[17]

Does not this suggest the need for systems thinking to conceptualize the firm as a system of connected activities? So why not begin with a holistic view of the firm? This point can easily be missed by those who observe desirable capabilities of firms and then build a theory of the firm solely upon those observations. However, a firm's culture that nurtures and sustains a collaborative knowledge-building proficiency is the fundamental cause of those desirable capabilities. David Teece, the principal architect of the dynamic capabilities theory of the firm, argues that capabilities are the cause of knowledge building (organizational learning):

Effective organizational learning—a continuous process in most industries—requires dynamic capabilities. These capabilities are activities that can usefully be thought of in three clusters: sensing opportunities (building new knowledge), seizing those opportunities to capture value; and transforming the organization as needed to adapt to the requirements of new business models and the competitive environment.[18]

Teece points out that ordinary capabilities entail doing things right whereas dynamic capabilities focus on doing the right things while adapting to a fast-changing economic world. Who can disagree with doing the right things? However, ask "How did capability X originate and improve over time, and we return to knowledge-building proficiency?"

The Agency Theory of the Firm

With their influential 1976 article, "Theory of the Firm: Managerial Behavior, Agency Costs and Ownership Structure," Michael Jensen and

William Meckling explained the far-reaching consequences of the lack of alignment between principals (shareholders) and agents (managers).[19] Basically, an agency relationship entails one or more principals engaging an agent to act on their behalf, requiring delegating decision-making authority to the agent. Jensen had exceptional skill in dissecting for a broad audience the economic fundamentals of major corporate issues (e.g., takeovers). Jensen's analyses, rooted in agency theory, demonstrated how corporate decision-making could misallocate resources and how corporate governance could rectify it.

Jensen's contributions to a theory of the firm were rooted in viewing the corporation as a nexus of efficiency-generating contracts among employees, managers, customers, suppliers, and capital owners.

He emphasized that stakeholder theory was deficient in being unable to resolve conflicts between stakeholders.[20] However, Jensen argued that if management made decisions to maximize the firm's total value, then this same criterion could be applied to evaluate proposed outlays for stakeholders.

Agency theory explains the heated market for corporate control (takeovers) in the 1970s and 1980s in response to entrenched management who refused to recycle to shareholders cash flows that exceeded management's opportunities to invest at or above the cost of capital ("free cash flow" in Jensen's terminology). The takeover premiums approximated the gain to shareholders from previously foregone market value due to management's reluctance to recycle free cash flow.[21] Leveraged buyouts offer a striking example of productivity gains due to linking management pay to performance coupled with tight alignment between management and the owners—agency theory writ large. As to how CEO compensation is decided by boards, Jensen and his coauthors argued for more closely tying CEO compensation to stock prices. This has been criticized for leading to a relentless upward trend of (perceived by many) excessively large CEO compensation.[22]

With the academic motivation to publish mathematically elegant articles, it is not surprising that agency theory has evolved in two directions: (1) highly mathematical and nonempirical "principal-agent" literature, and

(2) Jensen's "positive theory of agency," which minimizes mathematics and is empirically oriented.[23] Throughout his career, Jensen emphasized his strong preference for utilizing positive as opposed to normative research. Positive research seeks to better understand how the world actually behaves. Normative research asks questions that depend upon values (i.e., how an issue should be handled). Jensen reasons as follows:

> It is obvious from the logical structure of decision making that purposeful decisions cannot be made without the implicit or explicit use of positive theories. You cannot decide what action to take and expect to meet your objective if you have no idea about how alternative actions affect the desired outcome—and that requires positive theory.[24]

In the last decade of his working life, Jensen partnered with Werner Erhard to develop a leadership course that spotlighted integrity as a necessary ingredient to workability (productivity). After the global market crash of 2007–2008, Jensen saw a need to go beyond narrow self-interest in the management of firms. He noted: "I look forward to seeing the creation of an entirely new field of inquiry in economics, and in its sister social sciences, focused deeply on the positive analysis of the role of values in evaluating the possible outcomes of human interaction."[25]

Erhard and Jensen considered employee performance as profoundly influenced by employee perceptions of the firm's culture, which in turn connects with the Pragmatic Theory of the Firm.[26]

The Pragmatic Theory of the Firm

The Pragmatic Theory of the Firm begins by clarifying the firm's purpose. The following four mutually reinforcing objectives constitute the firm's purpose and should be guideposts for management:

- Communicate a *vision* that can inspire and motivate employees to work for a firm committed to behaving ethically and making the world a better place.
- *Survive and prosper* through continual gains in efficiency and sustained innovation, which depend upon a firm's knowledge-building proficiency. Nothing works long-term if a firm consistently fails to earn its cost of capital.
- Work continuously to *sustain win-win relationships* with all of the firm's stakeholders.
- Take care of *future generations* with a commitment to ensure the sustainability of the environment. The early design stage of products and processes needs to focus on minimizing waste and pollution.[27]

Importantly, the Pragmatic Theory of the Firm includes three core beliefs. First, the above mutually reinforcing objectives should be adopted to define the firm's purpose. Second, maximizing shareholder value is best positioned not as the firm's purpose but as the result of a firm successfully achieving its four-part purpose. Third, sustaining a culture of knowledge-building proficiency is the critical determinant of a firm's long-term performance in achieving its purpose.

Failure to secure genuine clarity as to purpose has led to endless debates about capitalism, which in turn has obfuscated the firm's critical role as the engine of economic progress. These debates typically begin with one side asserting that management's sole purpose is to maximize shareholder value, thereby maximizing their own compensation (tied to stock price performance). And this results in a hyperfocus on meeting or exceeding Wall Street's quarterly earnings expectations to the detriment of building long-term value and benefitting all stakeholders.

The pragmatic theory is about the *connectedness* of the firm's purpose, its knowledge-building proficiency, its major activities, and its long-term performance, emphasizing (measurable) financial performance. Figure 1.1 illustrates the components of this theory.

Figure 1.1: Components of the Pragmatic Theory of the Firm

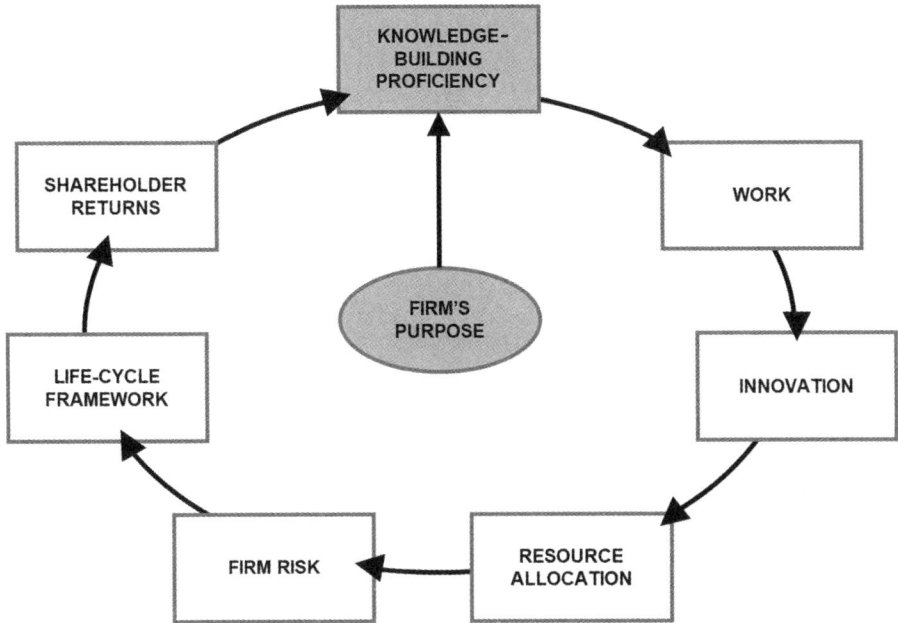

Source: Bartley J. Madden, "The Pragmatic Theory of the Firm,"
Journal of Applied Corporate Finance 33, no. 1 (2021): 98–110

Figure 1.1 highlights the firm's purpose as the beginning point for the Pragmatic Theory of the Firm. Achieving that purpose critically depends on integrating knowledge-building proficiency in the firm's major activities—work, innovation, and resource allocation.

Work

The Vanguard Method spotlights the need for systems thinking in organizing work and designing performance metrics useful for both management and employees. The objective is to reduce waste (i.e., time and resources spent that do not add value to the product/service). A systems perspective is essential in order to see how an action in one part of a system can cause waste in another part.

For example, management uses cost accounting to measure the efficiency of work being done and to determine productivity bonuses. Consider a manufacturing line where parts produced by A flow into B, where additional work is performed, and then proceed to C. The constraint (bottleneck) in the system is B, which has an excess amount of work-in-process inventory of parts waiting to be processed. To improve efficiency at A, a faster machine is installed. However, B is now swamped with parts to be processed. The result is a degradation of overall system efficiency stemming from a management action to improve localized accounting-based efficiency at A.

Systems thinking facilitates thinking about how value is created. Whether processing an insurance claim or building a windmill, proponents of lean thinking focus on the complete *value stream* for delivering the final product.[28] Picture an uncluttered value stream of horizontal flow across all activities needed to create value. However, for many firms, the picture shows a disjointed value stream cluttered with silos of functional activities connected to accounting-cost-based (local) performance metrics. These metrics in turn are connected to targets based on plans and budgets by which higher-level management seeks to control lower-level performance. As a practical matter, a theory of the firm benefits from a systems perspective that helps see performance in a way that connects the firm's major activities, including its organizational structure (analyzed in chapter 4) and related hierarchical control.

Consider lower levels in the firm where most of the value creation work gets done and where a knowledge-building culture is especially beneficial. Such an effective culture promotes continual improvement in employees' problem-solving skills, collaboration, and job satisfaction. This requires a work environment that treats problems as opportunities for improvement, plus the freedom to experiment and learn to the mutual benefit of employees and the firm. Moreover, in the spirit of win-win relationships, employees should participate in discussions that affect them. In such an environment, managers are skilled at asking the right questions. Toyota calls this thinking/behaving cultural process *kata*. Mike Rother, a leading expert on Toyota's culture, explains:

Toyota's improvement kata involves teaching people a stan-
dardized conscious "means" for sensing the gist of situations
and responding scientifically. This is a different way for humans
to have a sense of security, comfort, and confidence. Instead
of obtaining that from an unrealistic sense of certainty about
conditions, they get it from the means by which they deal with
uncertainty. This channels and taps our capabilities as humans
much better than our current management approach; explains a
good deal of Toyota's success; and gives us a model for managing
almost any human enterprise.[29]

Innovation

Knowledge-building proficiency involves constructive skepticism about
what we think we know. Our initial perceptions of problems and initial
ideas for new products can be hindered by assumptions that are no longer
valid but rarely questioned. Testing assumptions is the heart of innovative
designs of solutions that solve customers' problems and/or provide new
experiences that are valued by customers.

We can gain insights about the process of building useful knowledge
from design thinking. Design thinking is a process whereby participants
collaborate in order to repeatedly generate effective innovations. The
process involves prototypes, which are rough models of the key elements
of proposed designs. Importantly, prototyping helps refine what is possible
and desirable while staying in the bounds of technological constraints.
This serves as a reality check, an inspiration for new ideas, and a topic
for conversations that can generate a stream of asking better questions—a
prime source for breakthrough ideas. Design thinking relates to the
Pragmatic Theory of the Firm because innovation is a (subset) product
of a firm's knowledge-building culture. Let's review how Intuit, a premier
consumer and small business software firm, advantageously embraced
design thinking. (We analyze it later in this chapter using the life-cycle
framework.) In 2007, Intuit's management feedback showed competitors' product performance gaining on Intuit. In response, management

committed to moving beyond "designing for ease of use" of their software products to "designing for delight," or D4D. The point person for this initiative was Kaaren Hanson. Importantly, she worked with Scott Cook, Intuit's founder, who organized strong management backing. Over time, Hanson built a two-hundred-person team of innovation catalysts who were trained in design thinking and handled training. The catalysts were requested to devote two days a month for design work. This proved inadequate. Hanson summarizes:

> It used to be that we thought about doing design sessions for large-scale or strategic projects. But once we decided that our goal was really to get D4D into the company's DNA, the catalysts began to spend 90 percent of their time doing D4D in their *daily* work and 10 percent helping others outside of their core group to do design thinking. This was a very important shift, because when it was about the [training] sessions, people thought that design thinking is what you do in a one- or two-day period while someone holds your hand. But that's not really the big win. The big win is doing it in every meeting you're in.[30]

A significant proportion of Intuit's employees write software code or interact with customers, making experimentation and customer feedback less difficult. However, there is still a formidable challenge to improve commitment to deliver higher value to customers across the entire firm. This is about every employee participating in a continual stream of innovation. Those who neither write software nor interact with customers can think creatively and innovate in different ways to improve the efficiency of Intuit's many processes. Such a widely practiced culture constitutes a competitive advantage, enabling the firm to continually adapt using value creation as a guidepost and the nuts and bolts of design thinking as a toolbox.

Resource Allocation and Firm Risk

Resource allocation and firm risk are connected since management's resource allocation decisions involve either an explicit or an implicit assessment of risk. The traditional view of risk is variation from expectations with an emphasis on the magnitude of the potential downside deviation. However, management and boards that overly minimize the downside (we are in control) can easily forego the innovation and adaptation necessary to survive and prosper over the long term (one of the four objectives of the firm's purpose). This returns us to the beginning point for the pragmatic theory—the firm's purpose. Here is a definition of firm risk (see Figure 1.1):

> Firm risk is about obstacles management faces that interfere with achieving the firm's purpose. Firm risk increases (decreases) in lockstep with changes that degrade/improve the likelihood of achieving the firm's purpose. An *increase* in firm risk, all else equal, means a greater likelihood for a firm to generate *lower* future financial performance. . . . there can be a substantial time lag between a significant change in firm risk and investor perception of this change. As such, an increase in firm risk will eventually be understood by investors and, all else equal, this adjustment process will cause a decline in the firm's market valuation.[31]

In addition to conventional business risks, firm risk also includes less obvious ways that interfere with achieving the firm's purpose. Keep in mind that excessive management focus on meeting or exceeding Wall Street's quarterly earnings expectations can result in unethical and detrimental practices (e.g., cheating on automotive emissions testing). There are myriad ways that are not unethical but nevertheless undermine long-term survival and prosperity: not investing in employees by curtailing mentoring and training, neglecting high potential research and development (R&D) with a long-term payoff in favor of lower returns on R&D but having a quick payoff, etc.

In a fast-changing world, management needs to continually monitor if certain capabilities that previously contributed to a firm's competitive advantage have degraded. This may simultaneously offer new opportunities for value creation. But in the early stage of these competitive shifts, new opportunities are not visible, which is why questioning of assumptions and experimentation are so useful.

This happens by nurturing and sustaining a highly proficient knowledge-building culture that facilitates experimentation and fast adaptation to a changing environment. Such a culture typically resides in a firm with an organizational structure that promotes innovation with a minimum of bureaucracy. In contrast, firm risk increases with a culture ill-equipped for adapting to change due to business-as-usual attitudes coupled with heavy bureaucratic controls and an aversion to downside risk.

In general, resource allocation is justified to improve efficiency or expand product lines for businesses when expected returns on investment (ROIs) meet or preferably exceed the cost of capital. In addition, resources should be spent on exploring both new opportunities that use existing capabilities and new opportunities that require building or acquiring new capabilities. These exploratory investments can have a big upside yet be accompanied by a significant downside that warrants managing these opportunities like managing a startup business.

Here is a corporate governance principle that deserves to be etched on the wall of every corporate boardroom: Boards have the responsibility to evaluate the skill of business unit leaders and judge if they have earned the right to invest shareholders' capital. Shrinking a business unit and redirecting capital to more promising opportunities should be an alternative that is always on the table. What information do boards need to fulfill this responsibility? This is explained in the next section.

Life-Cycle Framework and Shareholder Returns

My involvement in the development of the life-cycle framework began in 1970 at an investment research firm, Callard, Madden & Associates.[32] Details of this work are presented in chapter 5. Today, many large money-management organizations worldwide use the life-cycle valuation model along with the global database provided by HOLT.[33] This section discusses how the life-cycle framework connects firm performance to stock market valuations and shareholder returns, an important capability that is missing from other theories of the firm.

The key life-cycle concept is that, in a market-based economy, a firm's economic returns (returns on capital) regress toward the average or cost-of-capital return. And its reinvestment rates (organic growth) slow as the firm gets larger and faces ever more competition. Figure 1.2 displays these relationships as transitional stages over a firm's life cycle.

Figure 1.2: The life-cycle framework

LIFE-CYCLE STAGES AND MANAGEMENT PRIORITES

High Innovation	Competitive Fade	Mature	Failing Business Model

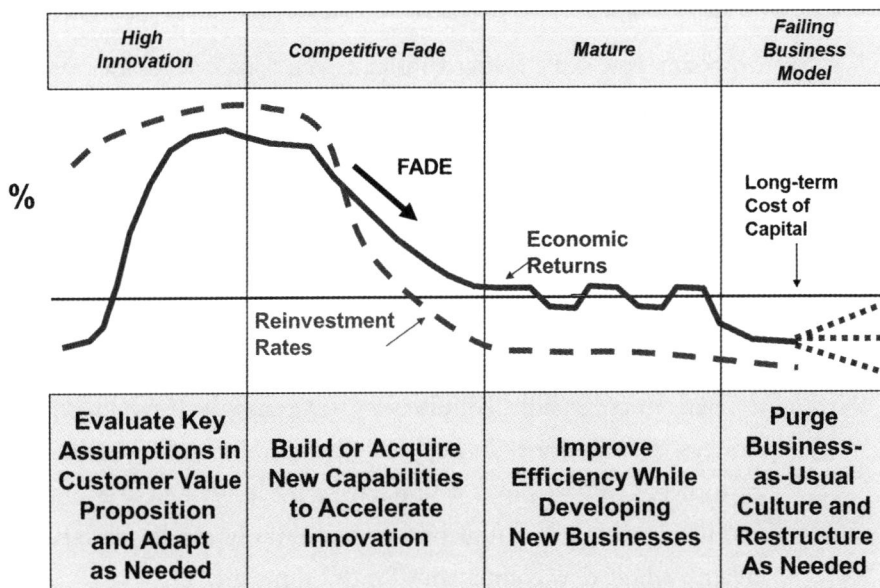

Evaluate Key Assumptions in Customer Value Proposition and Adapt as Needed	Build or Acquire New Capabilities to Accelerate Innovation	Improve Efficiency While Developing New Businesses	Purge Business-as-Usual Culture and Restructure As Needed

Source: Bartley J. Madden, "Understanding the Benefits of Capitalism through the Lens of a New Theory of the Firm," *Capitalism and Society* 17, no. 1, article 2 (2023).

At the *high innovation* stage, management's critical task is to confirm or refute key business model assumptions and, if necessary, pivot to a more viable approach to delivering value to targeted customers. High economic returns and high reinvestment rates are the hallmark of a commercially successful startup. Competitors are attracted to this opportunity and strive to duplicate and possibly improve upon the value creation offered by the successful startup. So begins the *competitive fade* stage.

As Figure 1.2 illustrates, the subsequent *fade* of economic returns (returns on capital) toward the cost of capital and slowing reinvestment rates quantify how the firm is performing relative to competitors. How can management achieve a favorable fade? The critical managerial task is to build or acquire the capabilities needed to expand beyond the comfort zone of their existing products/services. As noted earlier, the proficiency (or lack thereof) of the firm's knowledge-building culture helps or hinders in seizing new opportunities. Amazon's founding CEO Jeff Bezos succinctly describes the need to overcome a firm's comfort zone:

> Companies get skills-focused, instead of customer-needs focused. When [companies] think about extending their business into some new area, the first question is "why should we do that—we don't have any skills in that area." That approach puts a finite lifetime on a company, because the world changes, and what used to be cutting-edge skills have turned into something your customers may not need anymore. A much more stable strategy is to start with "what do my customers need?" Then do an inventory of the gaps in your skills. Kindle is a great example. If we set our strategy by what our skills happen to be rather than by what our customers need, we never would have done it. We had to go out and hire people who know how to build hardware devices and create a whole new competency for the company.[34]

At the *mature* stage, economic returns approximate the cost of capital, and management of the now much larger firm faces a tough challenge. There is a tendency to myopically focus on the efficiency of existing businesses; however, through experimentation with emergent opportunities—even though typically costly in the short term—management can position the firm to adapt early to fundamental change and possibly achieve economic returns on these new investments substantially more than their cost of capital. The hallmark of the *failing business model* stage is a business-as-usual culture that fails to adapt to fundamental change. Management perceives repetitive below-cost-of-capital economic returns as due to temporary economic conditions and other excuses. Purging this culture and shrinking the business is the top priority.

Traversing the Life-Cycle Stages: Eastman Kodak

The life-cycle track record for Eastman Kodak, 1960 to 2011 (see Figure 1.3), illustrates how life-cycle thinking provides insights in analyzing a firm's history. Note that historical analysis of financial variables requires adjustments for inflation to more accurately measure levels and trends. A common convention is to label inflation-adjusted variables as "real." The real long-term cost of capital for industrial firms in the US has averaged 6 percent.[35]

The top panel of Figure 1.3 plots economic returns with the real metric CFROI® (cash flow return on investment) that includes a considerable number of adjustments to minimize accounting biases (more details in chapter 5).[36] The dark horizontal line shows the benchmark real 6 percent cost of capital. The middle panel displays real asset growth rates that approximate (organic) reinvestment rates. The lower panel plots a relative wealth index that measures outperformance or underperformance of shareholder returns compared to the S&P 500.

A deep understanding of how best to meet customer needs (knowledge building) is the beginning step in value creation. In the late 1800s, George Eastman worked at a bank during the day and spent his evenings developing a way to overcome the technical headaches faced by professional photographers. His dry plate emulsion innovation clearly advanced the crude status quo process. He continually innovated and obsoleted his early work with a revolutionary camera designed to make photography available to everyone. It had film inside, and he called it the "Kodak." The Kodak camera was designed to be part of a *customer-friendly system* enabling customers to send the camera with its exposed film inside to Eastman's firm and receive back developed pictures and a fully reloaded camera. This was a value-added experience that the firm touted as "You press the button, we do the rest."[37]

Kodak dominated the film and camera market for decades and then, in the early 1960s, introduced the Instamatic cartridge, which greatly simplified loading and unloading film. CFROIs then surged to a 12 percent level by the mid-1970s (top panel of Figure 1.3). This was accomplished with significant real asset growth (middle panel). This unexpected surge in performance was rewarded by a rising relative wealth line (bottom panel) as Kodak's stock price outperformed the S&P 500. Then, from its peak in the mid-1970s, Kodak's future was all downhill. Why?

Kodak's core problem was a bloated and complacent bureaucratic culture emblematic of the failing business model life-cycle stage. A series of CEOs were unable to address the issue of a slow-moving firm in what had become a new world of fast-paced change. With improved quality, Fuji film became a formidable competitor to Kodak's film. Meanwhile, management spent R&D on improving yesterday's technologies. Even though digital photography originated at Kodak, it was ignored by management because they viewed themselves as running a film business. Management failed to anticipate the onslaught of cameras in cell phones.

As Kodak's march continued through the mature stage to the failing business model stage, management pursued an endless stream of acquisitions, divestitures, and restructurings culminating in massive layoffs and demoralized employees. Kodak filed for bankruptcy in 2012.

Boards of directors should position their firm and each of its business units on the life cycle. This pinpoints the current challenges and what should be the top priorities for management (see bottom of Figure 1.2). Life-cycle track records are especially useful in explaining the firm's current stock market valuation and past shareholder returns. As chapter 5 explains, future shareholder returns are driven by future life-cycle performance relative to life-cycle expectations at the beginning of the time period. A long-term fade upward of economic returns is rarely expected due to the skill required and almost always is accompanied by substantial outperformance of the S&P 500.

Figure 1.3: Eastman Kodak 1960–2011

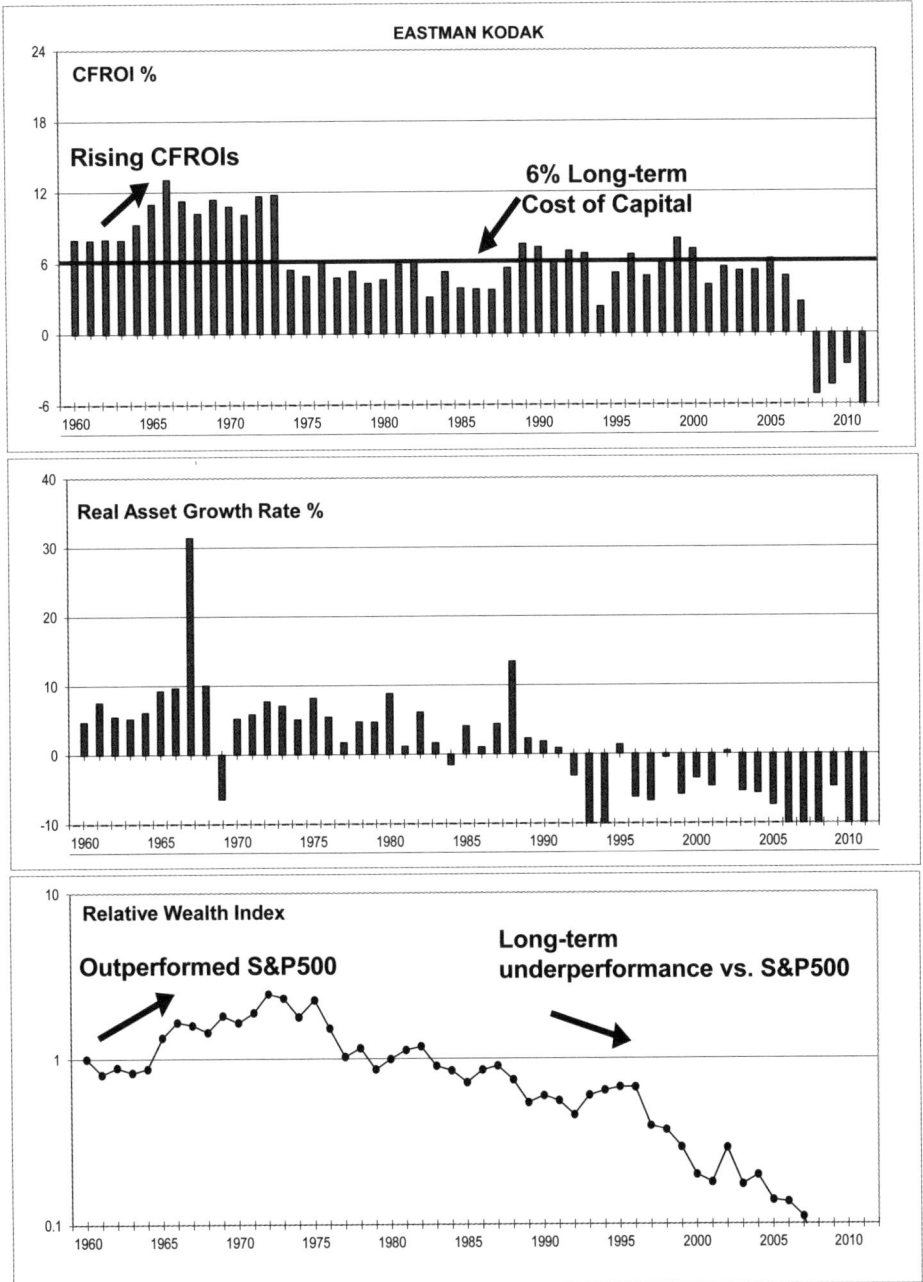

Source: HOLT Global Database

The Importance of Social Norms

Historical analysis of firms invariably involves understanding the firm's culture, as described by Edgar Schein:

> The culture of a group can now be defined as a pattern of shared basic assumptions learned by a group as it solved its problems of external adaptation and internal integration, which has worked well enough to be considered valid and, therefore, to be taught to new members as the correct way to perceive, think, and feel in relation to those problems.[38]

A firm with an effective knowledge-building culture promotes the questioning of assumptions, experimenting, and solving an array of problems necessary to implement value creation ideas. For such a culture to thrive requires a supportive organizational structure wherein employees enthusiastically contribute their knowledge to help other employees solve problems, with the realization that over the long haul everyone benefits from such collaboration.

Social norms play a critical role in a firm's culture. Social norms are about doing right and consistently being a member in good standing with society (e.g., fairness, reciprocity, honesty, and trustworthiness). This is ignored in neoclassical economics and in the agency theory of the firm that stresses rational self-interest.[39] Along these lines, top academic journals in accounting and finance continue to be influenced by the research paradigm promoted in Milton Friedman's famous essay, "The Methodology of Positive Economics," in which he asserts: "The only relevant test of the *validity* of a hypothesis is comparison of its predictions with experience."[40] In many instances of complex economic phenomena, much can be learned by organizing and studying data as if certain assumptions were valid. However, proponents of Friedman's positive economics often defend their models by asserting that their assumptions, which can be clearly unrealistic, are nevertheless not to be criticized—only pay attention to how well the model predicts. Hence, rational self-interest (a critical assumption) dominates model building while minimizing the importance of social norms.[41]

In contrast, Doug Stevens and I argue that the Pragmatic Theory of the Firm with its four-part purpose that includes win-win relationships must (and does) embrace social norms.[42] This also fits with firm risk that increases with the firm's unethical behavior, especially when widespread and condoned by management as a practical means to hit quarterly performance targets.

The firm is a system, and understanding its complexities requires multiple perspectives that extend far beyond the homo-economicus model, as recommended by Colin Mayer in this chapter's opening quote. Claus Dierksmeier acknowledges that there has been a reorientation in economic and business theory toward an appreciation of the social sciences and the humanities:

> After about 200 years of imitating the methods of the natural sciences and their thoroughly positivistic approach, and after decades of relegating any and all moral considerations to the margins of business theory, often belittling its tenets as not amenable to quantitative models, now, arguably, a paradigm shift is under way. We are seeing an ever stronger (re-)orientation of economic and business theory towards the social sciences and the humanities, and we are witnessing the return of qualitative methods and ethics to economics. . . . Management education, having inched away from the *homo economicus*-model for several years now, is about to cut loose fully from its former moorings in the mechanistic paradigm of the past. Instead of tracking the behavioristic depictions of human behavior as a mere pursuit of profit maximization, a new course has to be chartered. . . . To understand human agency, we must penetrate the normative dimension of the human mind. *Descriptions* of economic behavior match reality only when they are observant of the moral *prescriptions* that inform said behavior.[43]

Figure 1.4 showcases how shared essential social norms promote both a shared purpose and a knowledge-building culture. This is exhibited by employees who work hard to help other employees solve their problems without any immediate recognition or economic incentive, but simply because such behavior is the right thing to do and benefits everyone in the long term.

The importance of social norms and knowledge-building practices to a firm's culture is apparent when studying firm histories. Couple that way of thinking with the life-cycle framework, and the resulting lens is significantly more insightful than conventional security analysis keyed to earnings per share growth rates. Let's revisit Intuit and analyze its long-term performance in value creation.

Figure 1.4: Management and long-term performance

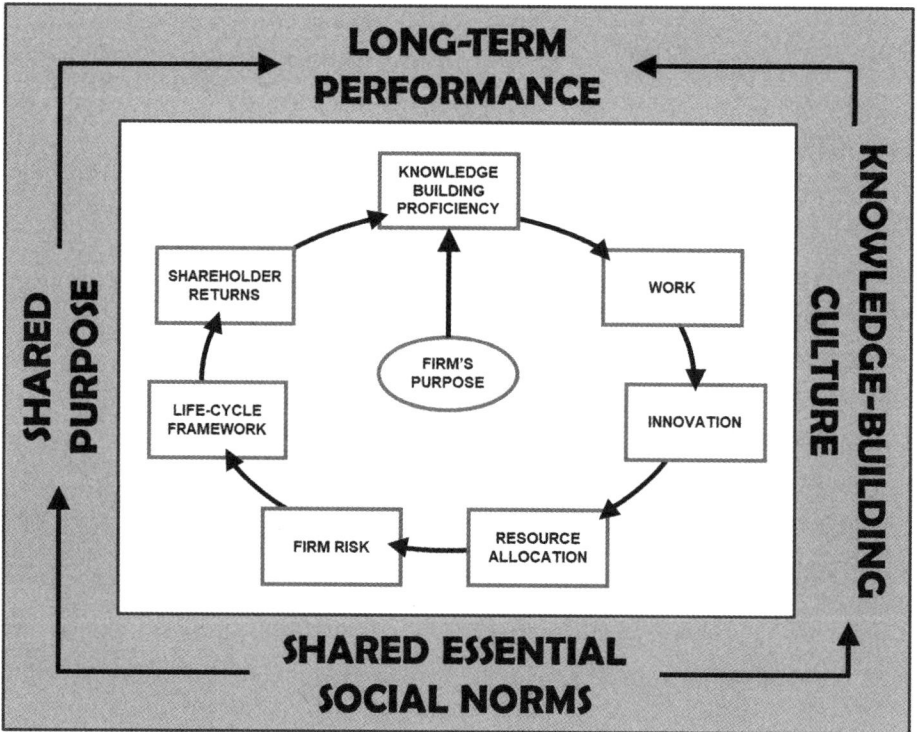

Source: Bartley J. Madden and Douglas E. Stevens, "Extending the Pragmatic Theory of the Firm with Social Norms," *Journal of Applied Corporate Finance*, forthcoming 2025.

Sustained Innovation: Intuit

Earlier in this chapter, Intuit's innovation skill in financial software for personal use and for small businesses was highlighted. The firm began in 1983 when cofounder Scott Cook envisioned personal computers replacing tedious paper-and-pencil personal accounting. Figure 1.5 displays Intuit's long-term life-cycle track record.

The steep drop in CFROIs (top panel) in the early years accompanied by exceptionally high reinvestment rates (middle panel) is not uncommon for a startup that is experimenting with its business model and trying to deliver superior value to its customers. In these early years, Intuit faced intense competition from Microsoft for both Quicken (personal finance) and QuickBooks (small business). The remarkable surge in CFROIs that was then sustained echoes the firm's proficiency in knowledge building. Shareholders were rewarded as the stock outperformed the S&P 500 tenfold (bottom panel) from 1993 to 2023.

Intuit beat Microsoft in the marketplace. How? In their book, *Inside Intuit: How the Makers of Quicken Beat Microsoft and Revolutionized an Entire Industry,* Suzanne Taylor and Kathy Schroeder noted an important detail about product development for Microsoft versus Intuit:

> Microsoft hired usability experts who ran the (product usability) tests and then produced a report . . . Microsoft engineers did not learn firsthand by observing customers interact with their software. In contrast, Intuit engineers loved to find problems with the software and treasured those "Aha!" moments when they watched a customer get stuck and realized, "My God that's so obvious; we did that wrong!"

Intuit's culture was summarized by Brad Smith, CEO from 2008 to 2018:

> Job one in creating a culture is building a purpose-driven culture . . . At Intuit, our mission is to improve our customers' financial lives so profoundly they can't imagine going back to the old way . . .

Figure 1.5: Intuit 1992–2024

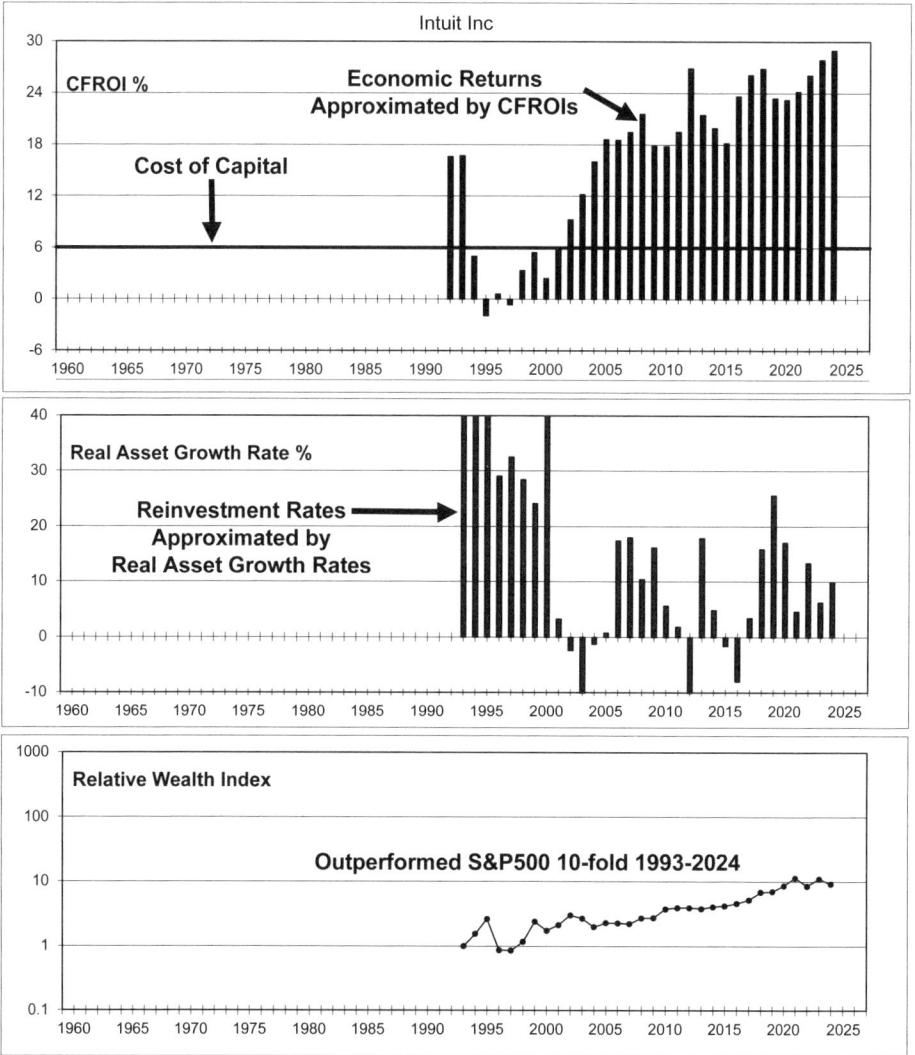

Source: HOLT Global Database

one way that leaders can create an action-oriented environment is to match inspiration with rigor, adopting a rapid-experimentation culture. Great ideas are simply hypotheses unless matched with tangible proof they deliver meaningful impact. A rapid experimentation culture cuts through hierarchy (especially if leaders hold their own ideas to the same scrutiny of testing), creating an environment where everyone can innovate, and "debate" turns into "doing."[44]

This quote neatly ties into the pragmatic theory's emphasis on purpose and the firm's knowledge-building culture. The CEO's words reflect the soul of Intuit. In contrast, typically Wall Street analysts myopically focus on quarterly earnings, which facilitates writing repetitive reports forecasting next quarter's earnings. Lost is an analysis of the culture that drives long-term value creation.

Intuit exemplifies the earlier point that (for economic progress) the most important type of organization is the company. It is the means to focus attention on the pain points encountered by people, whether or not they are current customers, doing a needed task. Minimizing those pain points leads to value creation.

As another example, Intuit's management green-lighted a project to help poor Indian farmers whose biggest pain point was perishable inventory that went unsold or had to be sold at a very low price. The new product, Mobile Bazaar, was quickly (mostly by word of mouth) adopted by 180,000 farmers who then realized significantly higher prices—an example of economic progress that lifts all boats.[45]

In conclusion, this chapter provides insights about systems thinking, highlighting its application by the Vanguard Method for service firms. We showed that the Pragmatic Theory of the Firm is rooted in viewing the firm as a holistic system with interrelated components: purpose, knowledge building, work, innovation, resource allocation, firm risk, and the life-cycle framework for insights about stock market valuations and shareholder returns. The incorporation of social norms in the pragmatic theory sharply contrasts with assumed self-interest that is the driving force of agency theory, which unfortunately is widely taught in business schools. The next chapter analyzes the critical determinant of a firm's long-term performance—knowledge-building proficiency.

CHAPTER 2

The Knowledge-Building Loop

In order to see differently, we must first see *seeing* differently. This is important in a deep, lived sense beyond just the visual. After all, the world is in constant flux. What was true yesterday might not be true today, and this is truer than ever, for example, in the world of technology and business, where developments occur seemingly at warp speeds. Contexts are always changing, so our perception must change too. Getting a stronger sense of the principles of your own brain allows you to see how subtly past experience not only biases us, but creates us. Knowing this, you can learn to take ownership over your brain's apparatus and thus make *new* pasts that will change your brain's perception of future possibilities.[1]

—BEAU LOTTO

The Pragmatic Theory of the Firm discussed in chapter 1 makes the case for knowledge-building proficiency as the critical determinant of a firm's long-term performance. As such, we need a mental model of the knowledge-building process that can be used to better understand problem-solving and more broadly innovation—aptly labeled by Matt Ridley as the child of freedom and the parent of prosperity.

This chapter does so with the Knowledge-Building Loop serving as the mental model for the process of building new knowledge.[2] The role of each Loop component is explained and connected to related insights (quotes) from well-known experts in the knowing process. The connected components offer a visual mental model of the knowing process, which can facilitate efficient storage and retrieval of innovation experiences.

To illustrate the Loop's widespread applicability, we discuss how the Wright brothers taught the world how to fly. Analysis of their experience shows how to mentally map innovation, enabling your own creativity to "fly" no matter your occupation. To further illustrate the Loop's widespread applicability, the final section discusses academic criticism of the Lean Startup in order to provide new insights for studying entrepreneurship.

Components of the Knowing Process

Figure 2.1 displays the components of the Knowledge-Building Loop. The knowledge base contains assumptions of varying degrees of reliability. One's worldview is a part of, and a result of, traversing the Knowledge-Building Loop to achieve one's purposes. A worldview represents ideas and beliefs through which we interpret and interact with the world. As to perceptions, our brains store past experiences to facilitate predictions via analogy to the past. Language is perception's silent partner and can powerfully camouflage assumptions. Importantly, it offers an actionable pathway to uncover obsolete assumptions. The reliability of linear cause-and-effect thinking for nonliving things can lead to a false sense of confidence when applied to complex systems, including human behavior. Fast and effective traversing of the Knowledge-Building Loop provides useful feedback that enables one to become more proficient in taking actions that produce desired consequences. The Loop enables an intuitive understanding of the knowing process that promotes constructive skepticism about what you think you know. This is a way of being (seeing) that underwrites the life of a value creator.

Figure 2.1: The Knowledge-Building Loop

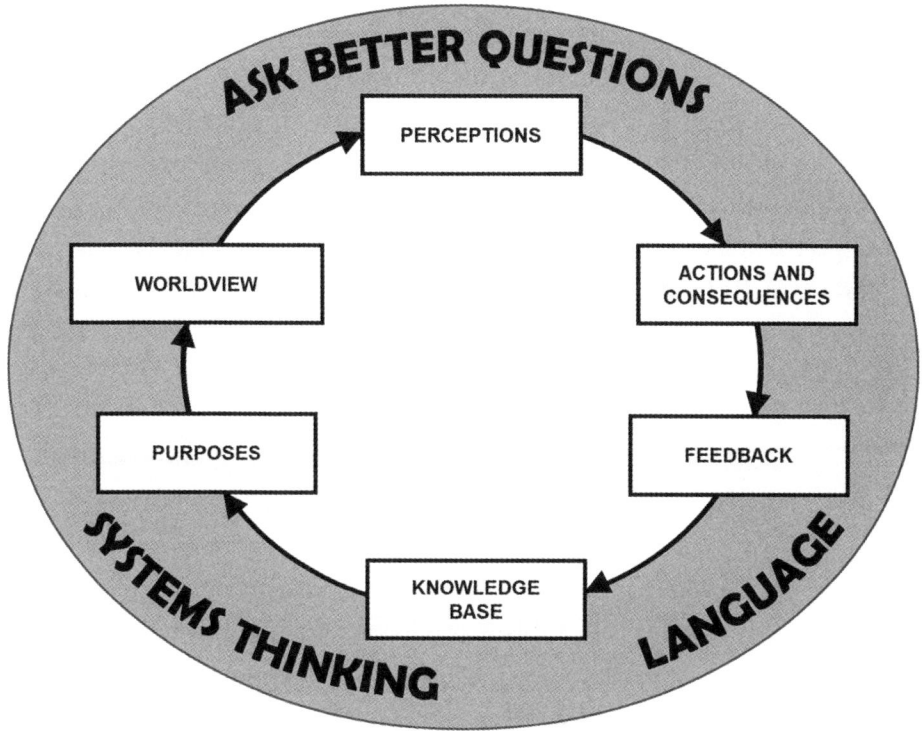

Source: Bartley J. Madden, *My Value Creation Journey: An Autobiography of My Work* (Naples, FL: Bartley J. Madden Foundation, 2024)

The quotes on the next pages provide different perspectives that support the logic for the connected components of the Knowledge-Building Loop.

Knowledge Base

Fast and effective traversing of the Knowledge-Building Loop is the hallmark of innovation, which requires humility about what we do not know. Fast and effective traversing also requires constructive skepticism about what we think we know and curiosity as to where different perspectives might lead.

Adelbert Ames's research on visual perception in the 1950s demonstrated the importance of past experiences in shaping our assumptions about the world. Ames argued that we do not perceive an objective reality but, rather, a useful representation constructed by our brains, which in turn is heavily influenced by our past experiences. This should encourage us to seek feedback (e.g., experiments and conversations with others who might have different backgrounds—different past experiences).

Consider Ray Dalio's complementary view of the process for improving one's knowledge base. He founded Bridgewater Associates—a highly respected money-management organization with superior long-term performance. He has been the firm's key architect of a culture that embraces constructive skepticism at all levels to benefit long-term performance. He discusses the knowledge-building process in his firm:

> Sincerely believe that you might not know the best possible path and recognize that your ability to deal with "not knowing" is more important than whatever it is you do know. Most people make bad decisions because they are so certain that they're right that they don't allow themselves to see the better alternatives that exist . . . open-minded people know that coming up with the right questions and asking other smart people what they think is as important as having all the answers. They understand that you can't make a great decision without swimming for a while in a state of "not knowing." That is because what exists within the area of "not knowing" is so much greater and more exciting than anything any one of us knows.[3]

Purposes

Purposes are critical to the process of taking actions, evaluating consequences, and learning (also unlearning), which is what knowledge building is all about. This process is keyed to actions and consequences—the practical stuff of lived experiences and not abstract philosophical principles. This resonates strongly with the pragmatism central to John Dewey's writings in philosophy. Interestingly, Dewey's support for individual participation in perceiving/knowing was later corroborated by Ames.[4] For

Dewey, the importance of the knowing process was tied to making better future choices. He believed that knowledge building was essential for freedom: "The only freedom that is of enduring importance is freedom of intelligence, that is to say, freedom of observation and of judgment, exercised on behalf of purposes that are intrinsically worthwhile."[5]

Worldview

Donella Meadows was a systems thinker, environmental scientist, and coauthor of the influential book *The Limits to Growth*. She warned of the tendency for linear analysis to break problems into small, understandable pieces, and then quickly settle on a presumed cause-and-effect relationship. Instead, Meadows focused on the structure of systems, clear understanding of system purpose, while exhibiting a deep appreciation for nonlinear relationships. Moreover, she believed that successful systems efforts to derive practical solutions must be grounded in a clearly defined problem. Also, one needs a commitment (i.e., worldview) to building knowledge, which, in turn, is based on interacting with others committed to systems thinking—easier said than done. Meadows was adamant about the need to overcome rigid worldviews that fail to evolve over time despite new learning.[6] She provides the following guidance:

> Keep oneself unattached in the arena of paradigms, stay flexible, realize that *no* paradigm is "true," . . . including the one that sweetly shapes your own worldview [and] tremendously [limits] understanding of an immense and amazing universe. . . . Everyone who has managed to entertain that idea, for a moment or for a lifetime, has found it to be the basis for radical empowerment. If no paradigm is right, you can choose whatever one will help to achieve your purpose.[7]

Perceptions

John Dewey viewed the connected process of past experiences—perceptions—actions—and new knowledge in the spirit of the Knowledge-Building Loop.[8] His thinking comports with leading-edge cognitive scientists such as Andy Clark, who wrote:

> Predictive processing is more than a new picture of perception. It is a new picture of action too. It displays them as co-constructed around the common goal of minimizing error in the prediction of sensory states. To perceive is to find the predictions that best fit the sensory data evidence. To act is to alter the world to bring it into line with some of these predictions. These are complementary means of dealing with prediction error, and they work together, each constantly influencing and being influenced by the other.[9]

Actions and Consequences

Matthew Syed, author of *Black Box Thinking: Why Most People Never Learn from Their Mistakes—But Some Do,* tells us that medical errors cause more deaths than traffic accidents, yet we lack a robust process for knowledge building to reduce such errors. In contrast, aviation crashes have a black box that orchestrates systematic knowledge building to eliminate the causes of past crashes. We benefit from embracing actions and consequences as a scoreboard where unintended consequences spark inquiry so that future actions produce desired results. Syed argues for a culture that acknowledges failures while willing to engage with them:

> The irony is that the social world is more complex than the natural world. We have general theories predicting the movement of the planets, but no general theories of human behavior. As we progress from physics, through chemistry and biology, out to economics, politics, and business, coming up with solutions becomes more difficult. But this strengthens rather than weakens the imperative of learning from failure. We need to come up with enlightened

ways of making trial and error [actions and consequences] effective through the use of controlled trials and the like, and be more willing to iterate our way to success. As situations become more complex, we will have to avoid the temptation to impose untested solutions from above and try to discover the world from below.[10]

Feedback

Beau Lotto is an entrepreneurial neuroscientist, founder of a neuro-design studio, Lab of Misfits, that aims to deepen our understanding of perception and human behavior, and the author of *Deviate: The Science of Seeing Differently*. A major takeaway from his book is that awareness of the principles by which your perceptual brain works enables you to become an active participant in your perceptions, so that you can change them in the future. By orchestrating different past experiences, including imagined futures, your brain can overcome automatic assumptions thereby opening up possibilities for different and more desirable futures. Lotto notes:

This is why trial and error, action and reaction (feedback) . . . namely, the "response cycle" . . . is at the center of perception. Engaging with the world gives our brain a historical record of experiential feedback that sculpts the neural architecture of the brain. That architecture and the resulting perceptions that ensue, are our reality. In short, our brain is history and little else . . . a physical manifestation of your past (individually, culturally, and evolutionarily) with the capacity to adapt to a new "future past."[11]

The Useful Habit of Dissecting Language for Hidden Assumptions

Words can be arranged in a logical sentence while camouflaging faulty/ obsolete assumptions. Language is so useful in our daily lives that we almost never question what assumptions our words are hiding. In that sense, language is perception's silent partner. In business, breakthrough ideas are generated by uncovering widely held faulty assumptions. In 2008, Joe Gebbia and Brian Chesky saw a big business opportunity lurking behind the phrase "hotel room." Their idea of renting privately owned residences to serve as hotel rooms led to the hugely successful company Airbnb.

Lera Boroditsky is a cognitive scientist and professor in the fields of language and cognition. Her research has focused on how the languages we speak operate at a foundational level in the brain's perceptual process. Boroditsky describes the early motivation for her work:

> I thought that languages and cultures shape the ways we think, I suspected they shaped the ways we reason and interpret information, but I didn't think languages could shape the nuts and bolts of perception—the way we see the world. That part of cognition seemed too low-level, too hard-wired, too constrained by the constants of physics and physiology to be affected by language. . . . I was so sure that language couldn't shape perception that I designed a set of experiments to demonstrate this. . . . I had set out to show that language didn't affect perception, but I found exactly the opposite. It turns out that language meddles in very low-level aspects of perception and without our knowledge or consent shape the very nuts and bolts of how we see the world.[12]

The Useful Habit of Systems Thinking

As discussed in chapter 1, a system is a group of interacting components that form a unified whole with a purpose. For example, a firm, which is a group of interacting components, operates within a broader system (economy). Systems increase in complexity with nonlinear relationships, feedback loops, and time-lagged effects driven by multiple causes. The dynamic behavior of a system makes understanding/predicting difficult. And enabling a system to achieve its purpose is not simply a matter of optimizing local efficiencies (components) given their interdependencies.

John Sterman, an MIT professor, carries on the tradition for systems thinking originated by MIT's Jay Forrester. In his book, *Business Dynamics:*

Systems Thinking and Modeling for a Complex World, Sterman lays out the logical thinking behind the modeling of complex systems in order to create the equivalent of "management flight simulators." The latter enables one to experience the effects of decision-making and to build knowledge to improve system design. He makes this important point:

> A fundamental principle of systems [thinking] states that the structure of the system gives rise to its behavior. However, people have a strong tendency to attribute the behavior of others to dispositional rather than situational factors, that is, to character flaws rather than the system in which these people are acting. . . . The attribution of behavior to individuals and special circumstances rather than system structure diverts our attention from the high leverage points where redesigning the system or governing policy can have significant, sustained, beneficial effects on performance. When we attribute behavior to people rather than system structure the focus of management becomes scapegoating and blame rather than the design of organizations in which ordinary people can achieve extraordinary results.[13]

The Useful Habit of Asking Better Questions

Think of how many projects of yours that start with answers and not questions—the opposite of how highly skilled architects and large-scale project managers successfully deliver creative and effective solutions. Think of hierarchical corporate organizations where promotions are based on skill in delivering results that meet or exceed, rarely questioned, specified targets.

Steven Shapiro led Accenture's consulting practice for fifteen years. His experience is grounded in producing practical solutions to problems, often involving reframing of problems and asking better questions. He emphasizes the importance of asking better questions:

> One word in a question can have a huge impact on the thought process and therefore on the range of solutions. For example, when

NASA was addressing the challenge of dirty clothes in space, they found one word made all the difference. Asking, "How can we get clothes clean?" yielded solutions around cleaning fluids. But "How can we *keep* clothes clean?" provided different responses. In this case, the solution became a material science problem involving clothing with built-in antimicrobials. Questions are powerful. And the words we choose for them are critical, because changing just one word can completely change your answers.[14]

Upgrading Creativity

A prerequisite to discussing creativity is a basic knowledge about how our brains work. Cognitive science supports the following takeaways:

- We see with our brains, not with our eyes.
- Our brains make judgments about what is important now to create sensible narratives—we see the world in terms of our ability to act.
- Perception depends upon intelligent guesswork (predictions) by our brains that are energy efficient and rely on past experiences stored in our memories.
- The goal of perception is to assess answers that are good enough for immediate survival—usefulness trumps accuracy.

Discussions about how our brains work and how we perceive the world can easily take a philosophical turn and get mired in debates about objective reality, free will, and consciousness. However, our concern in this book is the practical benefits from implementing insights about the knowing process, which includes our participation in shaping perceptions of reality.

For example, let's revisit the early 1970s when Kmart (then part of the S. S. Kresge Company) was the number one retailer in the United States. Kmart management extolled a business model that was rooted in stores operating as independent entities relying on store managers (close to the customer) handling merchandise ordering. To Kmart management, the reality was that the future would be like the past. Meanwhile, Sam Walton started Walmart and saw "reality" differently. He sensed that lurking behind the word "store" was an obsolete assumption. In contrast to a store as an independent entity, Walton defined a store as a node in a network—which changes everything.[15] Huge efficiency gains would follow from strategic placement of stores and warehouses and centralized ordering of merchandise. Kmart was eventually forced into bankruptcy after multiple CEOs were unable to compete at scale against Walmart.

Creativity is a function of the size of your brain's memory bank and your ability to retrieve relevant memories and to make novel connections for the problem/project at hand. In order to promote survival, our brains are motivated to store experiences that can explain something that might be helpful in the future. William Duggan has authored multiple books on developing a foundational process for creativity. He writes:

> The new science of learning and memory reveals at last how creative ideas form in the mind. When you do something yourself or learn what someone else did, those details go into your memory. When you face a new situation, your brain breaks down the problem into pieces and then searches through your brain for memories that fit each piece. It then makes a new combination from those pieces of memory. The combination is new, but the elements are not. These three steps—break it down, search, combine—are very different from the conventional steps of analyze and brainstorm.[16]

Making connections from your memory bank is the fuel for your imagination to create a mental model of something that doesn't yet exist.[17]

Fast and effective traversing of the Knowledge-Building Loop can generate highly effective solutions to everyday problems. More importantly, the probability of generating novel or even breakthrough creative ideas increases with constructive skepticism of what we think we know. And the probability of uncovering faulty (obsolete) assumptions increases with experimentation, networking, curiosity about inconsistencies and outliers, and a concern for system structure that may hold the key to change that dissolves many existing problems and/or avoids problems in the future. Asking better questions goes hand in hand with awareness that language is perception's silent partner. Hence, drill down to reveal the assumptions hidden behind the words.

Keep in mind that the end game for adopting the Knowledge-Building Loop as part of your problem-solving process is to upgrade your creativity in developing practical solutions to problems. It is plausible that the Knowledge-Building Loop facilitates storage and later retrieval of life experiences (including reading and conversations) that can prove useful for future value creation opportunities and for reframing of problems through awareness of the components of the knowing process (thinking about how one thinks). Hence, the integration of the Knowledge-Building Loop as part of your worldview quite possibly will upgrade your creativity.

Ideally, implementation of the Knowledge-Building Loop will lead to three habits shown in Figure 2.1: systems thinking, concern for language, and asking better questions. To see where an emphasis on language can lead, let's introduce L. David Marquet, captain from 1999 to 2001 of the nuclear-powered, fast-attack submarine USS *Santa Fe*. He led his crew from the fleet's worst-performing to the best-performing.

Upon taking command, Marquet realized that his authoritative, command-and-control leadership style was not going to work. That he lacked needed technical knowledge was immediately apparent to both himself and his crew. To his credit, he quickly struck a deal with the officers of the *Santa Fe*. Henceforth, he would not give orders as to what to do. Instead, he would provide intent as to what needs to be achieved. And crew members replaced "request permission to" with "I intend to," plus a widespread understanding that no one needs to be told what to do.

Marquet realized that he needed to replace an obsolete assumption in his knowledge base (i.e., that he knew what he wanted others to do). Furthermore, in its place, he believed that language was the key to improving overall system performance. Future performance of the *Santa Fe* verified that new assumption.

Marquet points out a faulty assumption with the command-and-control (top-down) approach to leadership: that there are leaders and followers. This can work in the short term. However, Marquet developed a belief in a leader-leader approach to running an organization (ship). So instead of moving information to authority, move authority to those with the information to achieve operational excellence (cause) that results in minimizing errors (effect). How so? Purging a culture of "just tell me what to do" improves problem-solving skills focused on eliminating a problem's root cause(s). To reduce recurrent problems on the submarine, the slogan adopted was "take deliberate action." The idea was to pause and think before taking action. On a nuclear submarine, this purposeful thinking proved highly effective.

The dramatic improvement in the performance of the *Santa Fe* is a stellar example of the power of language coupled with giving people the freedom to excel at their jobs. Marquet summarizes:

> Eventually we turned everything upside down. Instead of one captain giving orders to 134 men, we would have 135 independent, energetic, emotionally committed and engaged men thinking about what we needed to do and ways to do it right. This process turned them into active leaders as opposed to passive followers.[18]

How the Wright Brothers Taught the World How to Fly

Let's analyze the innovation journey of Wilbur and Orville Wright who, over a four-year time span using limited funds from their bicycle shop, were the first to successfully design and fly an engine-powered airplane. Neither brother had more than a high school education, but they grew up surrounded by books and with parents who encouraged curiosity. The Wright brothers' innovation process is neatly organized via the Knowledge-Building Loop.

Figure 2.2: Orville and Wilbur Wright

Interestingly, their existing *knowledge base* about bicycles proved to be a useful starting point for systematically building up new knowledge. Bicycles are inherently unstable until the rider learns how to control them. Their strongly held belief (assumption) was that control was the key to mastering flight. In contrast, their competitors viewed the challenge as building more powerful engines for a stable aircraft. In an 1899 letter to the Smithsonian Museum, Wilbur wrote, "I wish to avail myself of all that is already known."[19] Wilbur further noted: "It is the complexity of the flying problem that makes it so difficult. It is not to be solved by stumbling upon a secret, but by the patient accumulation of information upon a hundred different points, some of which an investigator would naturally think it unnecessary to go into deeply. This is why we think a quick solution impossible."[20]

As to *purposes,* the brothers viewed the primary goal of flying an engine-powered airplane as a knowledge-building task, which was the source of their competitive advantage (money was scarce for them). Competitors benefitted from being well funded compared to the Wright brothers, who built the first *Wright Flyer* for about $35,000 (in today's dollars). Moreover, since both brothers would be flying, an important *purpose* that permeated all of their activities was to avoid serious injury or death. This motivated their extensive experiments with low-risk gliders as a means of building knowledge. Obvious, you say. However, many of their competitors were big-idea designers who hired others to pilot their creations. Hence, pilot safety was not as crucial a purpose for them as it was for Wilbur and Orville.

One's *worldview* is highly personal and shapes how one sees the world. The extensive correspondence of the Wright brothers provides an excellent source for understanding their worldview.[21] They saw problems in terms of control, which inextricably led them to systems thinking. Their constructive skepticism about the work of others coupled to their own ideas represented a scientific lens for seeing the world. Orville summarized, "We had to go ahead and discover everything ourselves."[22]

For Wilbur and Orville, *perceptions* were guided by the overriding concern for pilot control. An early problem was that the use of rigid wings hampered control in general and especially when turning the airplane. Wilbur experimented with folding a long cardboard box. He flexed the box on both ends thereby altering its cross-sectional shape, observing that no damage resulted to the box. Wilbur made the connection that sections of the wings could be adjustable (this became known as wing warping) and restore equilibrium to the plane, along with increased control during a turn.

A hallmark of the Wrights' knowledge-building process was their reliance on experiments—*actions and consequences.* They discovered serious errors in widely accepted empirical relationships related to lift and drag. They constructed a small-scale wind tunnel with a wooden box and fan. Using miniature wing models, they ran extensive wind-tunnel experiments that generated far more accurate data. Orville noted:

> Earlier experimenters had so little accurate knowledge concerning the properties of cambered [asymmetry between the two surfaces of an airfoil] surfaces that they used cambered surfaces of great inefficiency, and the tables of air pressures . . . were so erroneous as to entirely mislead them. . . . I believe we possessed in 1902 more data on cambered surfaces . . . a hundred times over, than all of our predecessors put together.[23]

Feedback from their ingenious wind-tunnel experiments not only built up their knowledge base but was of immediate practical use in designing wings and a propeller. They imaginatively viewed a propeller as a wing traveling in a spiral course. The culmination of their knowledge-building journey was the construction of the *Wright Flyer.* One of their historic flights on December 17, 1903, was recorded on camera (Figure 2.3).

Figure 2.3: Success—December 17, 1903

In a statement to the Associated Press, Wilbur and Orville affirmed that their primary goal was achieved and said, "We packed our goods and returned home, knowing that the age of the flying machine had come at last."[24]

Figure 2.4 documents the pragmatic ways of implementing systems thinking that enabled Wilbur and Orville to systematically increase their knowledge base, all the while gaining confidence that their process would achieve the goal of powered flight.

Figure 2.4: Traversing the Knowledge-Building Loop

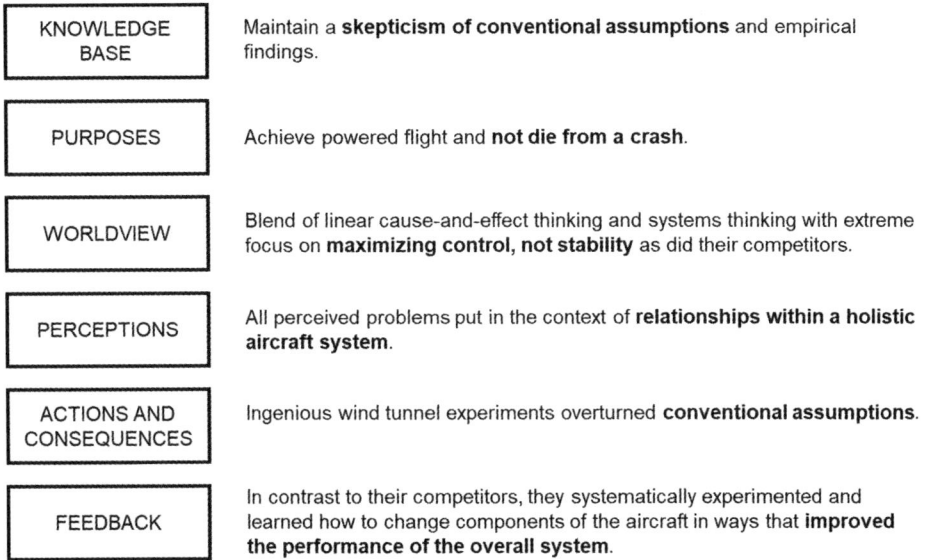

KNOWLEDGE BASE	Maintain a **skepticism of conventional assumptions** and empirical findings.
PURPOSES	Achieve powered flight and **not die from a crash.**
WORLDVIEW	Blend of linear cause-and-effect thinking and systems thinking with extreme focus on **maximizing control, not stability** as did their competitors.
PERCEPTIONS	All perceived problems put in the context of **relationships within a holistic aircraft system.**
ACTIONS AND CONSEQUENCES	Ingenious wind tunnel experiments overturned **conventional assumptions.**
FEEDBACK	In contrast to their competitors, they systematically experimented and learned how to change components of the aircraft in ways that **improved the performance of the overall system.**

The above figure summarizes insights as to how the Wright brothers excelled with all the Knowledge-Building Loop components. The next chapter applies the thinking of this chapter to practical problem-solving.

CHAPTER 3

Defining the Problem and Developing a Solution

It is often difficult for leaders to imagine a different world. It is this failure of imagination that so often leads to strategic surprises. . . . It is crucial . . . that data that challenge embedded orthodoxies be presented along with information that supports the common view. Otherwise . . . people will continue to do business in the echo chamber of their existing assumptions.[1]

—RITA MCGRATH

Designing a house, setting up a manufacturing process, or improving the effectiveness of a customer call center all involve defining problems and developing solutions. While on one level a business is operated to provide value to customers, on a deeper level a business is organized to effectively define problems and develop solutions.

This chapter focuses on approaches to problem-solving that are connected because they use variations of the Knowledge-Building Loop. Most definitely this is not a comprehensive review of the subject. Rather, an eclectic visit that I find fundamentally sound and deserving of attention: imagination, design thinking, logic trees and McKinsey's consulting road map, lean thinking, active learning and getting the value proposition right, lean startup, and functional fixedness.

Once viewed as the purview of artists, imagination is now recognized as being needed by businesspeople to conceptualize and solve our problems in a fast-changing environment.

Imagination

Martin Reeves and Jack Fuller succinctly describe the importance of imagination for business:

> For the sake of restoring the vitality of our companies, and for the societies these companies serve, we must better harness imagination. To imagine and realize new ways to meet collective and individual needs, companies must tap into the full humanity of the people who seek to work for them—the reward of which is sustained growth. . . . We are motivated by frustration at the declining creative capacities of mature companies and the aspiration that we can not only rehumanize our overly financialized and proceduralized corporations but put the human capacity for imagination at the center of collective enterprise.[2]

Imagination is the cognitive ability to assemble novel mental models of change to an existing object or process and to fruitfully explore the consequences, thereby improving the chances that the imagined change will achieve the desired practical result. Imagination improves with deep understanding—cause and effect and system interrelationships (i.e., systems thinking)—of the object or process coupled to constructive skepticism about what we think you know. The term "constructive skepticism" is reminiscent of Joseph Schumpeter's "creative destruction" in that both involve purging the familiar but now obsolete knowledge or process and replacing it with the new and improved.[3]

Constructive skepticism is another name for productive imagination. Skepticism leads to questioning assumptions that are often hidden by the language we use and may lead to a novel, eye-opening way of reframing a problem or even a breakthrough idea. Imagination needs to interact with the problem at hand so that doing and learning are mutually supportive. To sum up, imagination—fueled by systems thinking, attention to language, and asking better questions—facilitates fast and effective traversing of the Knowledge-Building Loop (learning cycles) as illustrated in Figure 3.1.

Figure 3.1: Imagination and the Knowledge-Building Loop

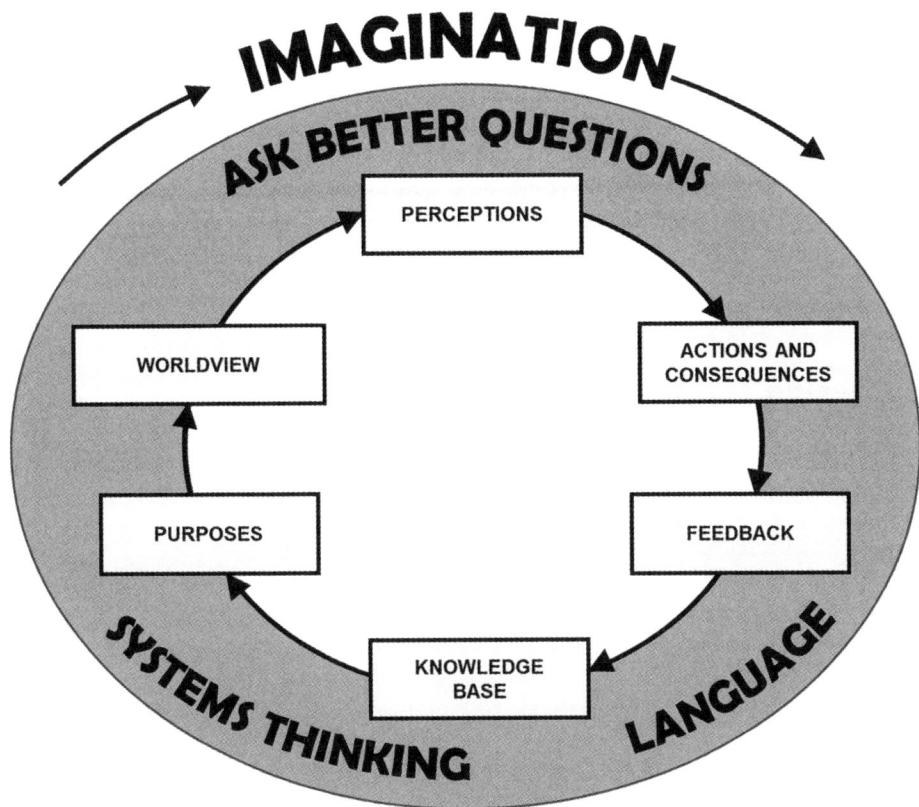

Imagination is about developing a novel approach for a problem situation and involves questioning of assumptions, mistakes, learning, and ultimately value creation. It is not just for the development of new products and services but is applicable for all the firm's activities (see chapter 1, Figure 1.1) such as performance measurement and nurturing a knowledge-building culture.

This tie-in between imagination and traversing the Knowledge-Building Loop resonates with Amar Bhide's discussion of entrepreneurs who have a skill for doubting, imagining, and justifying:

> Entrepreneurial ideas emerge from a creative process that combines facts and imagination. Entrepreneurs do not merely observe or notice facts. They imaginatively interpret what they observe or notice. . . . The innovative entrepreneur must imagine what could be and a possible path for getting there. . . . If sufficient information for logical or reliable statistical inference existed, there would be no opportunity for profit. . . . Imaginative justification and discourse are necessary to overcome the doubts that discourage hard-nosed investors from funding, astute employees from joining, and skeptical customers from buying the offerings of entrepreneurial ventures . . . the justifications must be *groundedly* imaginative.[4]

Design Thinking

Design thinking utilizes imagination to minimize a customer's significant pain points or to provide an entirely new and valued experience. Building prototypes—a critical component of design thinking—provides uniquely useful and fast feedback to expedite cycles of learning. Design thinking superbly exemplifies the Knowledge-Building Loop by feedback via prototypes and questioning of assumptions via deep anthropologist-like perceptions of customer behavior.

Consider managers of hospitals whose objective is to reduce medication errors. How best to accomplish it?

In an influential study, Amy Edmondson investigated two contrasting cultures in hospitals.[5] One was a tough-minded, high-blame culture in which nurses faced consequences for their medication errors. The other was a low-blame culture that focused on learning. Think of the two cultures as two different prototypes. The results from Edmondson's imaginative research design were striking. Nurses in the high-blame culture reported significantly fewer errors than the low-blame culture, but they did not report many errors because of a fear of consequences. Nurses in the low-blame culture were making fewer errors overall because they were experiencing fast learning cycles.

Edmondson's research underscores the potential insights from constructive skepticism of assumptions such as management's belief that actions leading to errors must result in negative consequences. Basic systems thinking suggests that the appropriate goal should be fast-paced learning that improves how work (taking care of patients) gets done. And that requires a positive feedback loop (i.e., reporting *all* errors results in taking better care of patients).

A holistic systems view of the firm is used in this chapter's discussion of imagination. This spotlights the connection between imagination and a knowledge-building culture, which, in turn, connects to other activities of the firm. Matthew Syed notes the critical connection between imagination and societal progress:

> Progress . . . is an interplay between the practical and the theoretical, between top-down and bottom-up, between creativity and discipline, between the small picture and the big picture. The crucial point—and the one that is most dramatically overlooked in our culture—is that in all these things, failure is a blessing, not a curse. It is the jolt that inspires creativity and the selection test that drives evolution.[6]

Logic Trees and McKinsey's Consulting Road Map

Two McKinsey veterans, Charles Conn and Robert McLean, coauthored *Bulletproof Problem Solving: The One Skill That Changes Everything* (2018). The book lays out the McKinsey approach to handling client engagements that entails defining the core problem and developing a practical *and* embraced-by-the-client solution. Dissecting this approach should be useful given McKinsey's long-term consulting success. Their book's blueprint can be distilled into a seven-step process:

- Define the problem consistent with the problem's context and boundaries.
- Disaggregate the issues and formulate hypotheses (logic trees are especially useful).
- Prioritize by locating high-impact levers and assessing the ability to move a lever.
- Develop a workplan for team members grounded in awareness of cognitive biases.
- Periodically stop the analysis and summarize the existing best understanding of the problem and solution.
- Synthesize the findings in a logically sound and compelling structure.
- Effectively communicate insights generated and recommended actions.

Logic trees disaggregate the problem and visually map in broad strokes relevant interrelated causes and effects. Logic trees facilitate asking better questions, utilizing a systems thinking view of the problem, and communicating to decision-makers the process of reaching a recommended solution. Systems thinking is useful for generating relevant questions that should first be answered before settling on the conceptualization of the problem. Moreover, systems thinking helps craft the problem by focusing on the gap between the current and the desired condition as perceived by the decision-makers. It is imperative to avoid a narrow definition of the problem that optimizes a part of a system but fails to optimize the whole system (overall firm).

The structure of the tree fits the context of the problem. (Helpful for many problems is to have the logic tree split [e.g., one branch for revenues and another for costs].) For example, suppose the problem is to decide if and when a client can profitably expand the productive capability of farmland. With a more detailed branch, we can observe crop revenues and, at another branch, crop costs. Say a particular crop has comparatively low total revenue, with high revenue per unit coupled with low cost per unit. At this point, the tree can be extended to identify what is involved with boosting total revenue for this specific crop—a possible leverage point. Solving a problem can lead to more refined logic trees such as detailed cause-and-effect analysis and trees that emphasize the formulation and testing of hypotheses.[7]

Conn and McLean are on board with the importance of analyzing assumptions:

> To disagree without being disagreeable is the heart of a great problem-solving team process. One of the great tools we both used in McKinsey is "What would you have to believe?" to accept a particular thesis or viewpoint. This involves spelling out all of the assumptions implicit in the perspective, and all the implications.[8]

The above quote resonates with the Knowledge-Building Loop's emphasis on language as an actionable pathway to discovering obsolete or faulty assumptions camouflaged by the words used—an underappreciated gold mine for developing novel, high-value ideas.

The McKinsey approach surmounts difficulties with the popular Five Whys approach that involves asking "Why?" five times to presumably arrive at the single root cause of a problem. The concern is with problems that manifest multiple causes. However, advanced versions of cause-and-effect mapping can reveal multiple causes for an observed undesirable effect. Causal loop maps of a process (system) are central to understanding how a system purpose or goal is achieved. Such understanding then becomes a prerequisite to making changes to solve a complex problem.

The more important and difficult a problem, the more useful is a skill in systems thinking. Along these lines, we next analyze lean thinking.

Lean Thinking

In their classic book, *Lean Thinking: Banish Waste and Create Wealth in Your Corporation*, James Womack and Daniel Jones emphasized that lean thinking is a stand-alone approach focused on five fundamental principles: "Precisely specify *value* by specific product; identify the *value stream* for each product; make value *flow* without interruptions; let the customers *pull* value from the producer; and pursue *perfection*." A successful lean culture operating throughout the firm will deliver high-quality products while minimizing waste (including time), thereby consuming less resources. Less waste translates to lower capital investment and manufacturing space.

The hallmark of a lean culture is knowledge-building proficiency at all levels of the firm. Interestingly, while Toyota is revered as the preeminent lean firm, Toyota veterans often suggest that TPS (Toyota Production System) should stand for Thinking People System to emphasize that lean is not a production system but an educational system.

Early on, Toyota jettisoned the assumption that low cost is solely achieved by high machine utilization. The key to achieving low cost is optimizing flow so that parts flow uninterrupted while minimizing waste. And that requires that employees continually improve their problem-solving skills. Lean thinking is about emphasizing flow in order to find the right problems while avoiding wasteful solutions.

Michael Balle and his coauthors provide insights:

> Lean thinking is at its core a different way of thinking about the development of capabilities that both shape and are shaped by strategy, about the role of leaders and managers to deliver it, and about the relationship between thinking and acting. Traditional business thinkers claim that strategy is a separate and more important thing than operations or organization, which they view as the mundane matters of how managers execute the strategic plan. . . . Lean thinking, in radical opposition, says that each shapes the other.
>
> The radical change proposed by a lean strategy is that by confronting his or her strategic intuition to obtain real firsthand facts experienced at customers' locations, at workplaces, and at suppliers, the leader expresses as challenges the top-level problems the organization has to resolve in order to thrive, frames the improvement direction to solve these problems, and expects each team to contribute controlled changes in order to form new

> solutions, sustained by a lean learning system embedded into day-to-day work. This approach creates both rapid and gradual change without disrupting operations or customer experience, and it also engages employees further in their relationship with their work, and the relationship of their work to customer satisfaction.[9]

The above quote reminds us of the usefulness of systems thinking and interrelationships (i.e., that strategy and operations, including the development of capabilities, can be viewed as mutually connected and shaping each other). This is an important idea.

Keep in mind that lean is people centric since it focuses on knowledge-building proficiency at low levels in the firm where work gets done. This is the path for employees to feel challenged, trusted, and recognized and to be able to continually learn while creating value and increasing their human capital.[10] Instead of a culture of managers orchestrating work-arounds to circumvent problems in order to make budgeted targets, a lean culture utilizes a scientific mindset for setting target conditions to improve components of a process and overcoming subsequent problems to achieve the next-level target condition. For example, excessive inventory is a result of a process that can be investigated by setting desired target conditions for components of the process. Solving the subsequent problems will reveal what created so much inventory. This is a bottom-up approach.

Lean has significant implications for a firm's organizational structure (discussed in chapter 4). Firms tend to be organized by departments and functions. However, this results in a lack of responsibility for the entire flow of value-added steps for a product or family of products. Optimizing not the silos of departments and functions but the overall value stream requires a dedicated manager. This person would be responsible for value-stream mapping that shows the current state and a (continually changing) desired future state. Two well-known lean thought leaders comment:

> Clearly, there is no end to the "future-becomes-present" cycle. This should be the heart of day-to-day management in any organization with a product to sell, whether it be a good, a service, or some

> combination constituting a solution to the customer's problem. As we've discovered again and again, when you remove sources of waste during a cycle you discover more waste lurking in the next cycle which can be eliminated. The job of lean managers and their teams is to keep this virtuous circle going. . . . Whenever there is a product for a customer, there is a value stream. The challenge lies in seeing it.[11]

In conclusion, value-stream thinking takes management beyond their own firm and deals with entire value streams that include suppliers and delivery to customers. The firm is a holistic system with connected activities. Sustained waste reduction and value creation are typically the result of actions that improve performance of the parts in ways that optimize the whole system.

Engaged Active Learning and Getting the Value Proposition Right

In 1988, Curtis Carlson became CEO of SRI International, known today for introducing world-changing innovations such as the computer mouse, electronic banking, robotic surgery, Siri, and HDTV. However, in 1988 the firm was at the failing business model stage, lacking a structured knowledge-building (innovation) process and in bad financial shape. Carlson's successful turnaround of SRI International was the result of a relentless focus on two essential steps for a sustained, productive innovation process.[12]

Step one: structuring the innovation process as *engaged active learning* (fast and effective traversing of the Knowledge-Building Loop). Step two: hyperfocused on *getting the value proposition right,* which has four interrelated components: (1) customer needs, (2) the chosen approach, (3) benefits relative to costs, and (4) comparison to competitors. The appeal of this two-step way of thinking is its pragmatic conciseness.

Typical specifications of a value proposition fail to adequately address all four of these components. There are three common mistakes:

- Innovators falling in love with their "big idea" and its role in the chosen approach
- Over-reliance on what customers say they want
- Excessive spending on an ill-defined approach

Carlson cautions about the widely believed assumption that startups benefit from quickly building minimally viable products (prototypes):

> *If the value proposition is not well-defined, building a minimally viable product wastes time and money.* At the start, the smallest possible team should be assembled to address the major risks in the value proposition. Until those risks are mitigated, building the offering is almost always a costly error.[13]

Furthermore, Carlson provides a vivid contrast between an abstract value proposition versus a concrete proposition:

> [A] team's value proposition identifies a need for a novel drone for bird-watchers and says the overall consumer drone market generates several billion dollars in annual revenue . . . another team [delivers a more useful proposition]: There are 20 million active bird-watchers in America who spend almost $30 billion a year on equipment. Of that total, 1% are hardcore birders who buy the latest equipment and want to capture close-up images and videos of their experiences. The top 5% of spenders in that group of enthusiasts represent a potential market of $15 million a year for ultraquiet, camouflaged, bird-watching drones.[14]

Carlson's ideas are also useful when thinking about other approaches to an innovation process, such as the Lean Startup discussed in the next section.

The Lean Startup and Breakthrough Ideas

Steve Blank, a serial entrepreneur, developed the original thinking for the Lean Startup and later communicated his ideas in the classroom.[15] Eric Ries, one of his students, embraced this framework and subsequently authored a bestseller, *The Lean Startup*, which was instrumental in promoting this framework worldwide. Others have also contributed to advancing the Lean Startup.[16]

For early-stage startups, Lean Startup avoids business plans that showcase long-term financial forecasts based on nothing more than aspirations and hope. Instead, it favors intense interaction with customers and showing them product prototypes (minimum viable products) plus the coordination of organizational capabilities with product development. The emphasis is on *actions and consequences* generating *feedback* that can quickly reveal faulty assumptions leading to the next iteration of knowledge building. When a core assumption is invalidated, the founders need to pivot and adapt their emergent business model to utilize discovered customer insights, thereby avoiding wasteful commitment of resources.

In a 2024 article, Steve Blank and Jonathan Eckhardt summarized their view of the Lean Startup:

> The primary task for the entrepreneur is knowledge generation. Entrepreneurs are advised on (1) how to uncover knowledge that helps them determine if a market exists that they can serve profitably by introducing a product or service, and (2) how to build an organization [Business Model Canvas] to serve a market, if discovered.[17]

Blank and Eckhardt recognize the value of the big idea. Moreover, they view the Lean Startup as deserving of more integration into entrepreneurship research. Less enthusiastic are Teppo Felin and his coauthors. While recognizing the Lean Startup's practical contributions, they have evolved an alternative (theory-based approach) that, in their view, overcomes significant shortcomings of Lean Startup:

> We view the central limitation of lean startup as its tendency to orient entrepreneurs toward ideas and products that can *quickly* and transparently be tested with customers. . . . The most valuable entrepreneurial ideas are those that are *un*likely to permit an easy, immediately recognizable experiment . . . and require some kind of contrarian belief, vision about and commitment toward a counterfactual world that may not easily be recognizable by other market actors.[18]

Proponents of the theory-based approach emphasize how the perceptions of entrepreneurs are influenced by the theories they are engaging, which directly connects to the discussion in chapter 2 on reality and perceptions.[19] They argue for early specificity of the contrarian belief/big idea.

The theory-based approach begins with what problem(s) must be solved in order to make a contrarian belief true.[20] This translates into a need to rigorously formulate the problems to be solved and design relevant experiments to verify that solutions have been achieved.

In summary, both Lean Startup and the theory-based approach do not address *how* to generate the big idea (contrarian belief). The next section addresses ideas that can help improve how people in general, and entrepreneurs in particular, generate the elusive but attainable *aha*—the big idea.

Functional Fixedness

Innovation generates a new value experience for customers. Significant gains in value creation typically involve creativity, which often is viewed as a novel combination of existing concepts. Before going deeper into the idea of combination, we need to be clear about what is being combined. In his book, *Entrepreneurial Valuation: An Entrepreneurial Guide to Getting into the Minds of Customers,* Mark Packard adeptly clarifies the definition of innovation:

> Scholars have argued that all innovations are new combinations of existing concepts that spark new ways of thinking about things. . . . new combinations generate new knowledge and implications. . . . The problem with this notion of innovation as concept merging is that the *innovation* does not happen until the new, merged concept is given a *purpose* [solve a problem]. . . . the *type* of knowledge that is combined matters. . . . two types of knowledge that are combined in every innovation process: problem (or needs) knowledge and technical knowledge. *Problem knowledge* specifies the problem to solve. Without a problem, there is no innovation, as innovation is always a solution to a problem. *Technical knowledge* references one's knowledge of resources and their affordances. . . . Innovation, then, is the combination of knowledge about a problem to solve and knowledge about resources that have properties that can solve the problem.[21]

The beginning point for significant innovations is to develop a different belief from conventional assumptions—a belief that has the potential to generate much-improved customer experiences. One way to expedite the development of such a belief is constructive skepticism about your current assumptions (knowledge base) manifested in the definition of a problem of interest and a proposed solution.

- Carefully examine your purposes, worldview, perceptions, actions and consequences, and feedback.
- Put under the microscope how these steps in knowing shaped your existing knowledge base.
- Contrast your knowing process with how others with much different backgrounds build up assumptions that differ from yours.

In addition, ask a question with the potential to eliminate the problem instead of incremental progress, for example, the (chapter 2) question: How in space can we *keep* clothes clean (not *get* clothes clean)? Move up a level and use a systems perspective that may have easily been ignored due to excessive focus on optimizing a component of the system. And most especially, drill down to discover obsolete assumptions hidden behind words. These assumptions may have been valid for a context that is no longer relevant today. That language matters is a recurrent theme in this book due to its importance and its widespread underutilization by innovators/problem solvers.

Here is a big idea that warrants discussion: The arrival of AI software could help better utilize language as an innovation tool to overcome functional fixedness.[22] The latter is a cognitive shortcut our brains use to perceive an object consistent with the most common and useful purpose for which it is used.

Tony McCaffrey and Jim Pearson use the sinking of the *Titanic* as an example of potential lifesaving actions that were never perceived due to the functional fixedness of those in charge of saving passengers.[23] Other than the limited supply of lifeboats, apparently no other options were even considered. Topping the list: viewing the "iceberg" as a "floating surface" that could serve as a waiting platform till rescue boats arrived. Also, the wooden doors and tables in the ship could have been fastened into floating devices. So, too, for luggage trunks. In summary, seize innovative applications by overcoming the restrictive uses accompanying the names we assign to things.

McCaffrey described the need for innovation at a ski company—get rid of vibrations in the skis enabling sharper turns safely at high speeds.[24] The path to a solution began with carefully stating the problem as *reduce vibrations* in skies. An innovative solution for skis emerged from investigating a similar problem in violins (i.e., *reduce vibrations* in the strings to produce a better sound).

A generalized process could begin with an AI-generated list of synonyms for *reduce* and for *vibrations* that, in turn, produces a large number of phrases that can connect to AI search routines across databases, including the US Patent and Trademark Office database. After a human has set up the task for AI heavy lifting, the output would be analyzed by the human looking for the "Aha!" connection. In this example, an innovation for violin construction was well suited for solving the similar, yet different, problem of enabling sharper turns on skis. Aha moments in engineering are no different from those in business since they result from a strikingly different belief from conventional assumptions that can potentially yield big benefits to users (customers). AI software holds promise for doing the heavy lifting that would enable humans to generate aha moments at a faster pace.

In conclusion, the ideas discussed in this chapter have a common denominator in the useful habits highlighted in Figure 3.1, specifically nurturing the habits of dissecting language for hidden assumptions, systems thinking, and asking better questions.

CHAPTER 4

Organizational Structure, Culture, and Freedom

In the permissionless corporation, fast, inexpensive experimentation takes over from slow, involved analysis, enabling organizations to pounce on opportunities as they arise. And at a time when speed and adaptability, rather than predictability and consistency, are the main sources of competitive advantage . . . a model [organizational structure] that allows people close to the customer to make as many decisions as possible is valuable. Companies with three or four layers, faster problem-solving, and a permissionless mindset will outcompete traditional players with 10 layers and slow decision-making processes. In fact, though it may take time, we anticipate that organizations that operate in the traditional way will eventually cease to exist.

—RITA MCGRATH AND RAM CHARAN[1]

This chapter contrasts command-and-control organizational structures with flatter structures that are increasingly being adopted worldwide.[2] This chapter discusses the historical reasons for this trend while also offering life-cycle track records for the preeminent steel manufacturer Nucor (relatively flat structure since its beginning); the Haier Group, a large global firm that has evolved into a high-performing flat organization; and Bayer AG, a large diversified health care firm, which currently is dismantling its command-and-control hierarchy. After analyzing the lessons learned from these important firms, the chapter concludes by discussing the key objectives for high-performance organizational structure and the challenges in transitioning to a flat structure.

Command-and-Control Hierarchy

Here is a thought experiment. Your only investment is ownership in a single firm, but you can also select one thing for management to get right. What would that be?

My choice: a culture of knowledge-building proficiency that operates at all levels of the firm.[3] Such a culture is a key contributor to superior strategy, innovation, and execution. It also contributes to the achievement of the firm's four-part purpose—vision, survival and prosperity, win-win relationships, and taking care of future generations. Hence, the firm's organizational structure should be shaped to facilitate the nurturing and sustaining of a knowledge-building culture.

Today's command-and-control organizational structure began in the nineteenth century with AT&T, General Electric, and Standard Oil. In the 1920s, General Motors refined this approach with managerial layers tied to budgetary controls for business units operating in a mass production environment. This approach was based on three beliefs: (1) important knowledge about running a business is generated by top management, (2) budgets and targets are needed to incentivize lower levels of the firm to do what top management wants, and (3) employees at low levels are not to be trusted. All three beliefs are obsolete in today's fast-changing world where superior results depend upon intangible (employee-created) assets and not merely scaling up tangible assets. The alternative to command-and-control is a flat organizational structure.

Standard cost accounting, which is harmful to firms pursuing a lean business strategy, has its roots in command-and-control for mass production (chapter 3). Brian Maskell and Nicholas Katko describe how standard cost accounting interferes with continuous improvement, emblematic of lean organizations, such as Toyota:

> For a traditional mass production manufacturer, a standard costing system . . . works based on the assumptions of mass production. The busier its machines and people . . . the more money will be made. A standard cost system reinforces this assumption in the ways that labor and overhead costs are absorbed for inventory valuation purposes. High resource utilization ensures high overhead absorption, which transfers manufacturing costs from the income statement to the balance sheet, improving profits. . . .
>
> Lean companies make money by maximizing flow on the pull from the customer, not by maximizing resource utilization. . . . [and by] relentlessly eliminating waste to create available capacity to meet increasing customer demand—and generating more profits. . . . Operational performance in a lean company is measured by improvements in cycle time, productivity, quality, flow, and cost. Standard cost information does not provide any relevant performance measures in any of these areas. Indeed, standard costing systems provide information that motivates people to take actions that sabotage lean operational improvement.[4]

The first step in an accounting solution for lean-thinking firms is to adopt a value stream (system) mindset that sees production as a horizontal flow. Easier said than done. How top management thinks and the data they use can be formidable obstacles to nurturing and sustaining a lean business strategy coupled to a flat organizational structure.

Budgets: The Lifeblood of Command and Control

The lifeblood of command-and-control hierarchies is the budget that sets in motion the target marching orders for those at lower levels. Of course, budgets invariably lead to gamesmanship in setting lower forecasts of future performance, which are then easier to beat thereby earning a "performance" bonus.

When Bill Anderson was CEO of Roche Pharmaceuticals, he tried to overcome this gamesmanship and concomitant hoarding of resources by eliminating budgets. He purged targets and budgets and told everyone to serve patients and drive progress. The result was spending down and performance up. Anderson notes that Roche's vibrant culture and shared purpose gave him confidence that people would do the right things.[5]

The movement to eliminate budgets began in Scandinavia and has produced impressive results for many large European firms (e.g., Roche, Equinor). The approach is called Beyond Budgeting and is explained in a 2023 book, *This Is Beyond Budgeting: A Guide to More Adaptive and Human Organizations* authored by Bjarte Bogsnes. Note his careful use of language:

> A target is an *aspiration,* what we want to happen. A forecast is an *expectation,* what we think will happen, whether we like what we see or not. And resource allocation is about *optimization* of scarce resources. . . .
>
> Some tell me it is impossible to operate without a budget. My response is that this separation lets us do everything the budget tried to do for us, but now in much better ways: better targets, better forecasts, and a more effective resource allocation. It also improves how we measure, evaluate, reward, and coordinate. How impossible and scary is that?[6]

In the following sections, three firms are discussed to illustrate sharply different journeys to jettison outdated and unwieldy command-and-control structures.

Nucor and Employee Freedom

Nucor is the preeminent steel producer with the highest productivity and highest-paid employees (teammates) that produces high-quality steel at the lowest cost. Management has sustained a flat organizational structure (four layers of management from the CEO to employees working in the steel mills) and culture (win-win partnerships, team bonuses tied to productivity, and no layoffs) nurtured by Ken Iverson, CEO from 1965 to 1996. Iverson was a smart risk-taker who bet big and early on mini-mills that use recycled steel and thin-slab casting—innovations that led to long-lived core competencies.

In their especially insightful book, *Humanocracy: Creating Organizations as Amazing as the People Inside Them,* Gary Hamel and Michele Zanini tell two stories about Nucor employees that spotlight flat organizations at their best—autonomy, freedom, transparency, communication/knowledge building, responsibility, and treating everyone as a value creator.

First, Nucor's Hickman, Arkansas, unit was exceptionally profitable for many years supplying steel tubes for oil and gas drilling/fracking during a period of sharply rising oil/gas prices. When the trend in prices reversed, Hickman's profit turned into losses. A Hickman team focusing on new opportunities uncovered two potentials: specialized steel for electric motors and high-strength steel for auto parts. To seize these opportunities, $230 million was needed for a large-scale mill expansion, and top management quickly secured the funding. This capital expenditure project was led by a former maintenance engineer.

Second, teammates at Nucor's Blytheville, Arkansas, unit analyzed whether their furnace should be replaced. Their analysis clearly showed the net benefit from replacement. Disappointed with the bids they solicited from furnace suppliers, they hired a fabricator and jointly developed a new furnace for one-tenth the price of the initial bids.

Keep in mind that historically the steel industry has generated miserably low (and cyclical) returns on capital. Let's look at Nucor's life-cycle track record from 1960 to 2023 (see Figure 4.1). The top panel displays inflation-adjusted CFROIs. Nucor generated cyclical CFROIs that averaged much higher than the cost of capital. The middle panel shows significant asset growth as Nucor expanded and earned a higher share of the steel market. Big Steel (U.S. Steel and Bethlehem Steel) with their bureaucratic, pyramid command-and-control hierarchies was unable to reorganize their business model and change the adversarial relationship with their unionized employees. By the way, Nucor has never had a union. The relative wealth index in the bottom panel records a cyclical but long-term rising trend as Nucor's stock outperformed the S&P 500.

Figure 4.1: Nucor 1960 to 2024

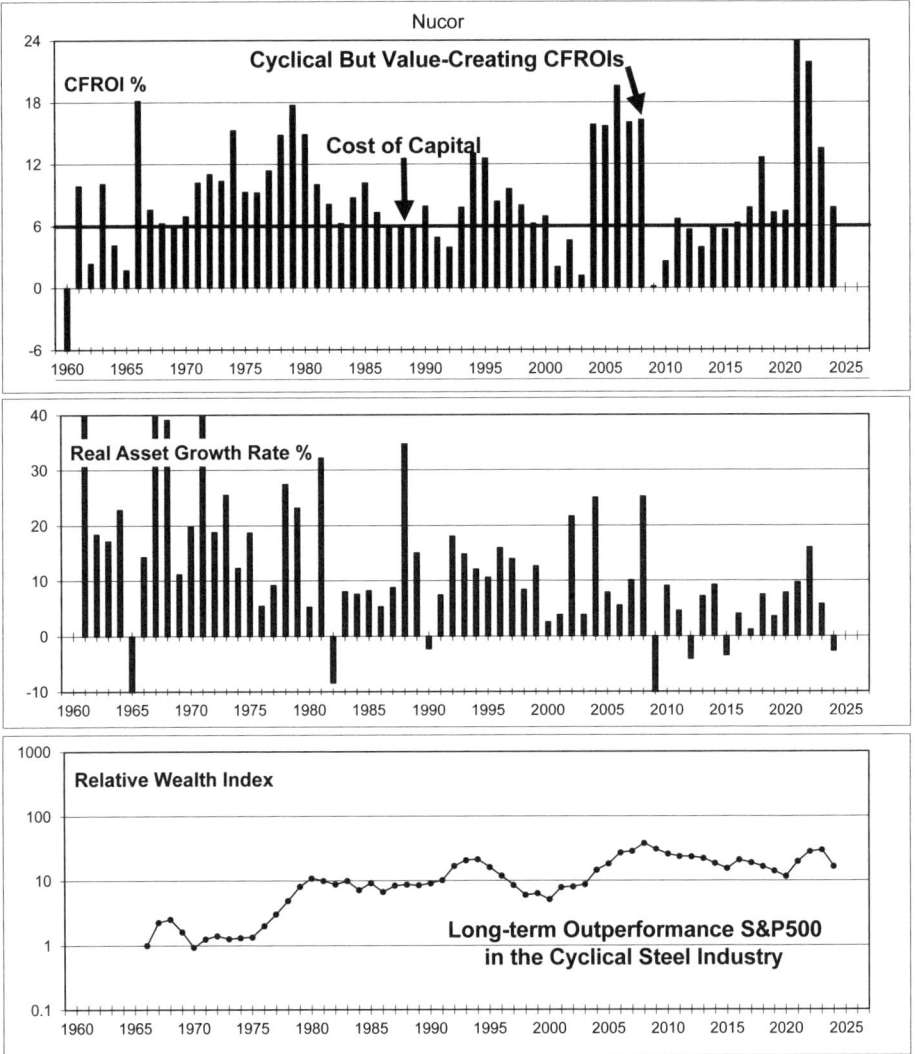

Source: HOLT Global Database

Here are key takeaways from Ken Iverson's autobiography, *Plain Talk: Lessons from a Business Maverick:*

- We anticipate that roughly half our investments in new ideas/technologies will fail.
- Our independent business units have an unusually active exchange of problem-solving ideas.
- We (management) have been able to get employees to identify their own interests fundamentally with management.
- We have no job descriptions. We let our employees define their own jobs in ways that optimize their productivity.
- Our business units are autonomous, and we accept the added cost from duplication since this eliminates bureaucratic control that comes with centralization—it works for us.
- If your success requires uniformity and consistency (McDonald's and Walmart), centralized decision-making may be required. But if success relies more on innovation and flexibility, push decision-making power lower.
- We built Nucor under the assumption that most of the "genius" in our firm is found among the people doing the work.
- We focus on shaping an environment that frees employees to determine what they can do and should do, to the benefit of themselves and Nucor.

Isn't the last bullet point the essence of freedom for those working in any organization?

Ken Iverson became CEO of Nucor when it was a mix of disconnected, mainly money-losing operations and then began a remarkable value creation journey to the benefit of all the firm's stakeholders. Similarly, Zhang Ruimin became CEO of Haier Group when it was on the verge of bankruptcy. His journey is discussed next.

The Evolution of Haier Group

A visitor to the Haier Group's corporate headquarters in Qingdao, China, will see a glass-enclosed sledgehammer mounted on the wall. This is a reminder of the beginning of a value creation journey for Zhang Ruimin when he became CEO in 1984 of Qingdao General Refrigerator Factory. This was a money-losing Chinese refrigerator manufacturer with eight hundred employees and clearly in the failing business model life-cycle stage (chapter 1, Figure 1.2). The level of employee morale was reflected in Ruimin's first new rule: Do not pee on the factory floor. As to product quality, Ruimin got employees' attention by using the sledgehammer on many defective refrigerators recently manufactured.

Haier became not only the global leader in white goods (refrigerators, ovens) but also a flat organization with thousands of microenterprises (MEs) that orchestrate the design, manufacturing, and delivery of unique customer experiences as part of an ecosystem-driven organization. The success of Haier's MEs is evidenced by many of them having been, or soon to be, spun out as publicly traded firms in a wide array of businesses.[7]

Ruimin evolved a management framework (philosophy) that he labeled RenDanHeyi to emphasize employees ("ren") committed to continually providing users ("dan") with superb value-creating experiences ("heyi"). RenDanHeyi aligns value creation for users and value sharing for employees. Haier is adamant about being exceptionally close to its customers to both understand/serve current needs and anticipate desirable future experiences. Haier calls this zero distance, achieved via Haier's platform networked to collaborating firms that contribute to the customer experience.[8] Danah Zohar, in her book, *Zero Distance,* notes that Haier does more than strive for zero-distance relationships. Haier broadly communicates customer problems and requests for ideas to hundreds of thousands of potential contributors (not just known experts). Successful contributors earn a share of profits, with some becoming leaders of new MEs. An ecosystem for sure, with Haier as the hub of a large multicompany network.

Zohar provides insightful details:

> When Haier first introduced RenDanHeyi, by dividing the company up into thousands of smaller micro-enterprises, it found that a kind of dog-eat-dog, zero-sum competition emerged between them. . . . soon . . . an ecosystem model of win/win cooperation was encouraged. MEs quickly learned that if they teamed

up to form temporary partnerships, they could offer more total solutions to users.

Its long-standing preference to aim for growing numbers of loyal customer numbers rather than concentrating on market share as a criterion of success. . . . Zhang Ruimin sums up this logic, "By fulfilling users' every need, we are cultivating life-long users that will stay with us."[9]

Haier's life-cycle track record (see Figure 4.2) displays Ruimin's value creation journey in financial terms. In early years (top panel), CFROIs declined below the cost of capital and the stock underperformed the market (bottom panel). The subsequent tenfold outperformance of the market was driven by increasing investor expectations for sustaining much higher CFROIs coupled to high asset growth rates (middle panel). That asset growth included the 2016 acquisition of General Electric's appliance division, which at the time was delivering anemic growth in sales. Five years later, after implementing the key elements of RenDanHeyi, sales had doubled.

Figure 4.2: Haier Group 2000 to 2024

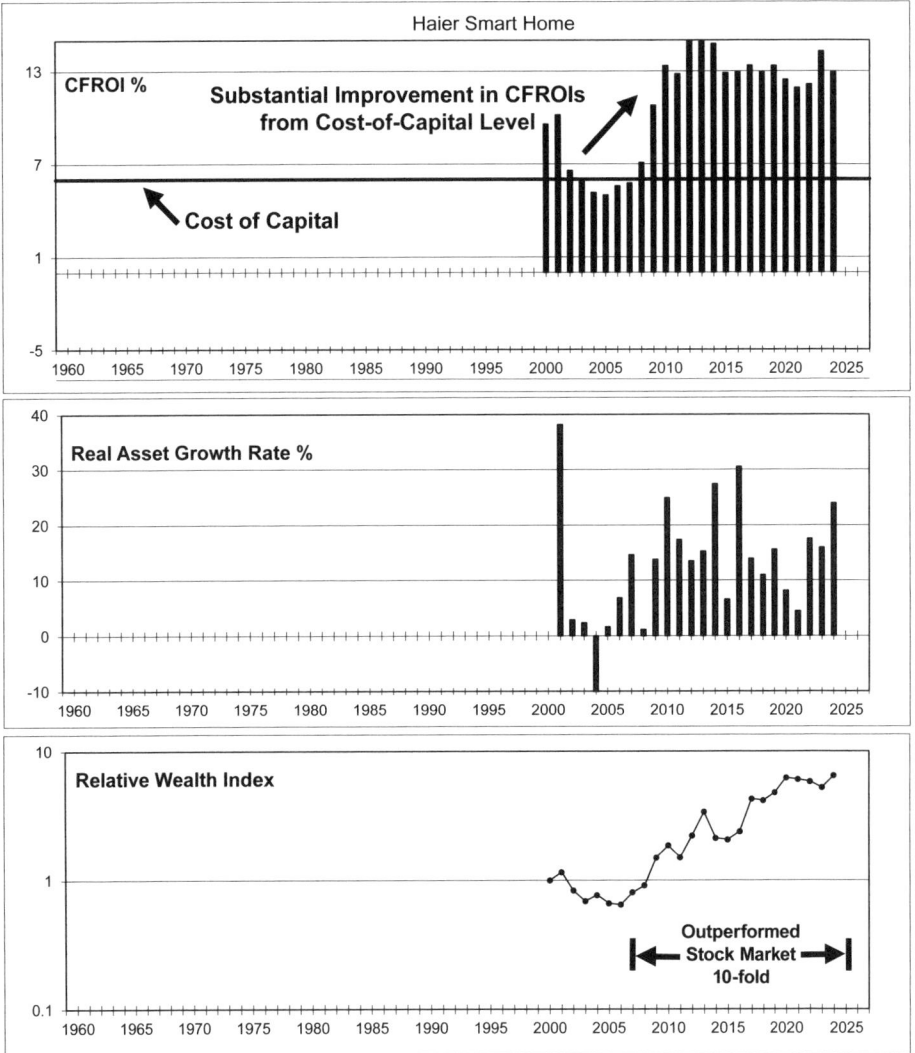

Source: HOLT Global Database

The final example of a transformation to a flat structure is Bayer, a large firm with a highly bureaucratic structure coupled to significant near-term problems self-inflicted by a disastrous mega-acquisition pushed by the former CEO.

Radical Restructuring at Bayer AG

Bayer AG is a German firm whose two major businesses were pharmaceuticals and consumer health when Werner Baumann became CEO in 2016. He immediately orchestrated a mega-acquisition to create a third major business, crop science. Bayer paid $63 billion, a significant premium to acquire Monsanto. This sharply increased Bayer's debt load and also bought ownership of tens of thousands of ongoing and future lawsuits claiming that Monsanto's Roundup herbicide caused cancer. Litigation costs skyrocketed. And coupled with interest on the debt load, pharmaceutical R&D fell short of what was needed to replace Bayer's top drugs coming off patents. Meanwhile, Bayer grew beyond one hundred thousand employees, all managed with a bureaucratic command-and-control organizational structure.

After intense shareholder pressure, Baumann resigned and Bill Anderson became CEO in mid-2022. (Recall our discussion of Anderson eliminating budgets when he was CEO of Roche.) Figure 4.3 shows Bayer's life-cycle track record.

Figure 4.3: Bayer AG 1982 to 2024

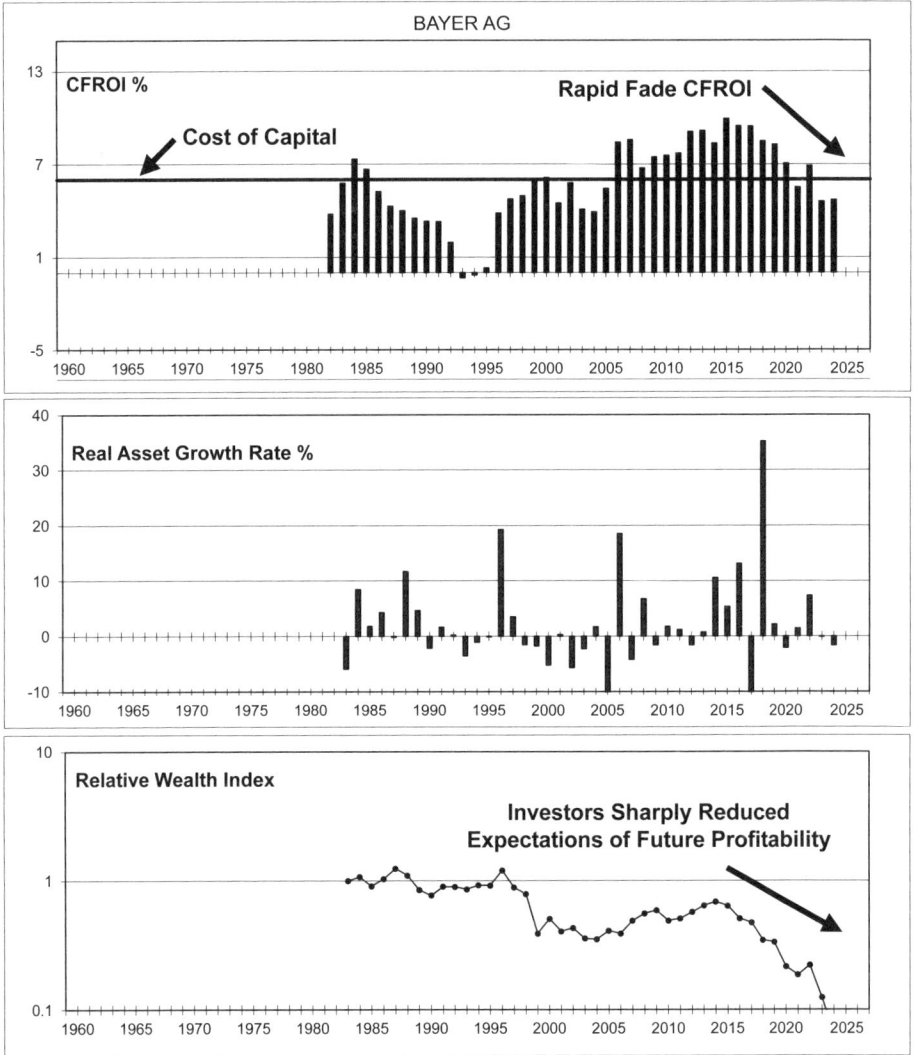

Source: HOLT Global Database

At the beginning of 2025, Bayer's equity market value was $20 billion. The top panel shows recent CFROIs below the cost of capital. The bottom panel shows the relentless lowering of investor expectations for future profitability beginning with the initial offer in 2016 to acquire Monsanto.

Recognizing the severity of Bayer's situation, the board supported Anderson's multiyear radical reorganization, which he named "Dynamic Shared Ownership." Commenting on the extensive bureaucracy spawned by Bayer's command-and-control structure, Anderson noted that Bayer's manual for company rules covered 1,362 pages. His 2023 letter to shareholders summarizes:

> Bayer has huge potential. But, as in many large companies, we often make life difficult for ourselves. There is a whole lot of coordination, monitoring and supervision going on. In some areas, we have 12 hierarchy levels between the CEO and the customer.
>
> Why is that a problem? Because this traditional approach of top-down management doesn't place products and customers at the heart of daily work. Decisions take far too long. Initiative and creativity are stifled by bureaucracy.
>
> That's why we want to turn our system on its head. In the future, 95 percent of the decision-making will shift to the people actually doing the work. We are introducing a new operating model, which we call Dynamic Shared Ownership. This new system will reduce hierarchy levels, eliminate bureaucracy and significantly accelerate decision-making. We will primarily work in small, self-managed teams, totally focused on improving our products and the lives of our customers. This shift will enable us to unleash the entrepreneurial power of each individual and ensure that all of our efforts are focused on the needs of consumers, patients, and farmers.

In a nutshell: Rapid decision-making occurs at lower levels, managers become coaches, and team-led innovation cycles typically span ninety days—teams are built around the customer (not the boss) and not around annual budget targets. As just one example of what a team of eight employees, with a variety of skills, recently accomplished: They reduced the time to launch a new product for women seeking to get pregnant, One A Day Prenatal Vitamins, from one year to ninety days.[10]

Anderson is leading the Bayer team to overcome significant short-term problems and to excel in delivering on Bayer's long-term vision: "Health for all, hunger for none." To execute this vision, Michael Lurie, point person for implementing dynamic shared ownership, remarked: "Instead of designing the organization despite what it means to be human, you design the organization around what it means to be human."[11]

Organize to Sustain a Fast-Learning Culture

The foundational purpose for a flat organizational structure is to promote a culture that facilitates fast and effective traversing of the Knowledge-Building Loop. Benefits accrue at all levels of the firm and include crafting innovative strategies, solving manufacturing problems, and facilitating feedback to accelerate product innovations. Recall in chapter 1 how in Intuit's early years, the firm's product developers orchestrated one-on-one customer feedback that was decidedly superior to Microsoft's process. This expedited learning cycle, which in turn identified often subtle customer pain points followed by iterations (design for delight) of design changes so that customers became avid Intuit users.

The absence of fast learning is one of the fundamental reasons for lengthy delays and skyrocketing costs for megaprojects, such as the construction of underground subway systems, high-speed rail transportation, and large-scale manufacturing facilities. This area's thought leader is Bent Flyvbjerg. He emphasizes in his article, "Make Megaprojects More Modular":

> I've researched and consulted on megaprojects for more than 30 years, and I've found that two factors play a critical role in determining whether an organization will meet with success or failure: replicable *modularity* in design and *speed in iteration*. If a project can be delivered fast and in a modular manner, enabling experimentation and learning along the way, it is likely to succeed. If it is undertaken on a massive scale with one-off, highly integrated components, it is likely to be troubled or fail. . . . Humans are

inherently good at experimenting and learning, which is why a
venture based on modular replicability is more likely to succeed
than one that depends on long-range planning and forecasting—
something humans are inherently bad at.[12]

An example of the opposite of fast learning cycles is large-scale one-
of-a-kind nuclear reactors in which most components are customized.
Unsurprisingly, the typical result is massive delays and skyrocketing costs.
However, where there are problems there are opportunities.

Small modular reactors (SMRs) are being developed (e.g., NuScale
Power, TerraPower) to minimize manufacturing/assembly delays and costs.
Also, due to their reduced complexity, expectations are for much quicker
approvals from the Nuclear Regulatory Commission. SMRs illustrate
the importance of bottom-up innovation by firms to achieve high-level
societal needs such as reduced emissions from electricity generation.[13] A
strategically well-positioned firm is BWX Technologies (BWXT), which
is the most experienced designer and manufacturer of nuclear systems,
partly due to designing and manufacturing the nuclear components for
all US nuclear submarines. In addition to extensive development of their
own SMR, other SMR developers look to BWXT as a preferred partner.

Tesla's Gigafactory 1, a large-scale manufacturing facility outside Reno,
Nevada, supplies lithium-ion batteries and electric vehicle components.
The planned capacity will make this the largest (manufacturing) footprint
in the world—large enough to house 107 football fields. Tesla management understands Flyvbjerg's insights about modular construction and
fast learning. With management's organization of work, after module
construction is completed, it becomes operational and produces a useful
component or product that does not need further downstream processing.
What is at work here is a parallel, not sequential, mindset for fast learning
cycles that reduce costs and accelerate revenue generation. Such a mindset
is broadly applicable to managing most any business.

This mindset focuses on thinking slow but acting fast. Meticulous and
time-consuming planning does not cost much but greatly reduces the risk
from acting fast. This mindset is evidenced by Ed Catmull's management

of the innovation process to produce movies for Pixar Animation, which has had an extraordinarily successful track record. Catmull emphasizes that he is not concerned with directors spending years experimenting with and addressing problems pinpointed by their peers. Detailed feedback from highly creative peers, who are motivated to help since they also go through the same process, identifies problems early. These development costs are low and pale in comparison to major changes to a movie when it is in full production. Catmull provides insights about achieving workability early on for strategy, communication, and a firm's organizational structure:

> We had made the mistake of confusing the communication structure with the organizational structure. Of course, an animator should be able to talk to a modeler directly, without first talking with his or her manager. So, we gathered the company together and said: Going forward, anyone should be able to talk to anyone else, at any level, at any time, without fear of reprimand. Communication would no longer have to go through hierarchical channels. . . . Figuring out how to build a sustainable creative culture—one that didn't just pay lip service to the importance of things [social norms] like honesty, excellence, communication, originality, and self-assessment but really *committed* to them, no matter how uncomfortable that became—wasn't a singular assignment. It was a day-in-day-out, full-time job. And one that I wanted to do.[14]

Ambidextrous Organizational Structure and Social Norms

Chapter 1 introduced the life-cycle framework (Figure 1.2) and critical managerial priorities dependent on a firm's life-cycle stage. Many large firms are close to, or headed toward, the mature stage, earning approximately cost-of-capital returns. The top priority at this stage is to continually improve the efficiency of the firm's existing assets while simultaneously developing new businesses with the potential to earn more than cost-of-capital returns. Allocating resources between exploitation (existing assets) and exploration (investments in new areas) is a difficult managerial challenge.[15] Michael Tushman and Charles O'Reilly disagree with Clayton Christensen's recommendation that oftentimes startup businesses should be spun out.[16] They want new businesses to be able to leverage existing capabilities. They argue:

> In contrast to Christensen's solution, we argue that leadership teams must be able to manage streams of innovations; they must be able to handle existing products and services even as they create new ones. Consider the difference between the alignments needed for a high-performance mature business with a well-known technology and processes, and those needed to succeed in a new emerging business with uncertain technology and rapidly changing markets. Clearly the two alignments are different and yet to succeed over long time periods organizations need to be able to do both: to compete in mature markets on the basis of cost and quality and to compete in new markets based on speed and adaptability. Successfully managing these multiple alignments requires that managers build *ambidextrous structures*—structures that have several distinct alignments simultaneously.[17]

Keep in mind that management allegiance to Wall Street's hyperfocus on meeting, or preferably beating, quarterly earnings expectations is an impediment to successfully sustaining an ambidextrous organizational structure. This is because nurturing new businesses in the short term is typically costly and thereby lowers quarterly earnings compared to not investing in these new opportunities. Management needs to demonstrate skill in developing new businesses and to communicate clearly why investments in these future opportunities are being made.

For example, a key to Amazon outperforming the market a hundredfold from 1997 to 2018 was Jeff Bezos's skill in not only developing new businesses (e.g., Kindle and the AWS cloud computing platform) but also his effective shareholder letters explaining why Amazon operates as it does. When Amazon's large-scale capital expenditures depressed quarterly earnings, often its stock price would increase simultaneously with the announcement of a "weak" quarter by Wall Street's standards. Investors grew to appreciate the firm's commitment to value creation over the long term and its exceptional skill in both running existing businesses and starting up new businesses.[18]

In their analysis of an ambidextrous organizational structure, Tushman and O'Reilly emphasize the importance of social norms—accepted attitudes and behavior (i.e., the right thing to do)—reflected in a firm's culture.[19] Recall the role of social norms in the Pragmatic Theory of the Firm (chapter 1, Figure 1.4). Social norms are an integral part of a firm's innovation process. This is expected since formal controls take a back seat to culture/ social norms in an environment of uncertainty, fast-paced change, and a learning process that builds upon mistakes. Tushman and O'Reilly developed an extensive research program that provides the following insights about social norms and innovation:

- Creativity is stimulated by support for risk-taking and change plus tolerance for mistakes.
- Nonmonetary rewards, such as recognition from management and colleagues, can be more effective than monetary bonuses.
- Tolerance for mistakes is critical and should be accompanied by clarity about acceptable types of risk-taking and mistakes.
- Norms that promote implementation of innovations include speed of managerial decision-making, teamwork, information sharing, adaptability, and personal autonomy.

A Practical Approach to Improving Organizational Structure

The usefulness of viewing the firm as a holistic system was discussed in chapter 1, which highlighted the Vanguard Method developed by John Seddon. He provides a condensed and insightful summary of essential objectives for a firm's organizational structure:

> Imagine an organization that is designed . . . [starting with] demand. It will be *customer-driven* because the customer is central to the design of the organization—the fundamental design would be outside-in (from the customer inwards) rather than top-down. . . . It will be *adaptive*, because it can respond naturally to changes in customer demands. Success will depend on the ability to learn about the "what and why" of current performance in ways that lead to knowledge and, hence, predictable improvements. . . . It will be a *system* because the point is to manage with understanding and knowledge of how the parts work together . . . the way the work works will be the mindset. . . . And last but not least, people have a sense of freedom. Freedom to act, learn, experiment, challenge—and build relationships with customers. Becoming a customer-driven learning system requires freedom, not command and control.[20]

The easiest way to nurture and sustain a structure similar to the above is to start a firm with an exceptionally talented CEO, such as Ken Iverson of Nucor or Zhang Ruimin of Haier, who understands systems thinking and the importance of freedom for motivating people to create value, and have them remain CEO for an extended period of time, during which the board of directors supports experimentation and change in the firm's organizational structure.

The above idealized situation does not apply to today's large command-and-control firms like Bayer prior to Bill Anderson becoming CEO. As noted earlier, Bayer is facing serious business problems having lost 80 percent of its equity market value from 2015 to 2024 as investors lowered their expectations consistent with the failing business model life-cycle stage. That big change was needed has led the board to green-light CEO Bill Anderson's radical initiative to transition to a flat organizational structure. This work in progress should yield useful insights for sure. Even if the Bayer reorganization becomes a resounding success, expect boards of large (one hundred thousand employees plus) firms to be especially cautious concerning significant change to the firm's organizational structure. So, what approach makes sense enough to gain board support?

A firm is a complex system. A change of organizational structure is a major shock to the system. Let's discuss seven perspectives to better understand what is needed to orchestrate a change that will, in fact, improve performance.

First, let's take the perspective of the leading critics of flat organizations, Nicolai Foss and Peter Klein. The essence of their argument is:

> The key challenge for designing and operating hierarchies today and tomorrow is to balance two opposing forces. The first is the desire, common to us all, for empowerment and autonomy, which helps companies mobilize employees' creativity and exploit their unique knowledge and capabilities. The other is the need—particularly in environments characterized by rapid change and interdependent activities across the enterprise—to exercise managerial authority on a large scale. . . .
>
> A central lesson of theories and evidence on organizational structure is that there are no universally best answers to these questions, only trade-offs that depend on the contingencies facing the company. Identifying and acting on those trade-offs—not decentralizing everything, everywhere—is the key to successful leadership. . . .
>
> In redesigning managerial authority and hierarchy for the 21st century, leaders must realize that they don't need to know everything, but only just enough, and they need to consider what their employees want and think is fair in designing structures and systems.[21]

Second, organizational structure is the design of a system to achieve a specified purpose (e.g., the firm's four-part purpose), with interdependent components that work together and comprise the whole. Should not a firm be organized (as discussed in chapter 3) consistent with a lean business (organizational) strategy, which, in turn, is an overarching strategy for purposeful thinking and acting? This ideal structure is highlighted in the above Seddon quote.

In the spirit of interconnected components that work together, a lean business strategy necessitates replacement of the standard cost accounting system, which was analyzed earlier in this chapter. This holds promise for a large-scale reduction in bureaucratic waste caused by an accounting system rooted in mass production independent of value creation. This is the big elephant in the room that rarely is recognized in analyses of organizational structure.

Third, proponents of lean/flat organizations extol the benefits of bottom-up strategic ideas from lower-level employees who are close to customers and are experienced in seeing waste and opportunities for value creation. Of course this is highly useful information. However, we should recognize that a skilled management will have a much broader view of the competitive landscape and emergent technologies than lower-level employees. This equips management to make key technology decisions even if early signs of technological shifts were first observed at low levels in the organization. Examples of such management decision-making include Andy Grove transitioning Intel from the production of memory chips to microprocessors, Ken Iverson's "bet the firm" decision for Nucor to lead the way in the steel industry with mini-mills that use recycled steel, and Jensen Huang of Nvidia making an early big bet on AI chips.

Fourth, context matters. In general, smaller and simpler firms are expected to more easily transition to a flat structure compared to larger, more complicated firms, especially those operating in a fast-paced technology environment. Proponents of a flat structure often showcase Morning Star and its high-performance track record and highly motivated employees (associates). We should note that Morning Star operates in the processing and packing of tomatoes, not noted for rapid technology change.

Fifth, management needs expertise in systems thinking, and that includes favorably positioning the firm in ecosystems to both create and capture value. Such decisions are best orchestrated at high levels of the firm.

Sixth, command-and-control organizations use accounting-based targets, budgets, and performance metrics to control lower levels to produce accounting results (earnings growth, return on capital) that are the planned objectives. Isn't a viable alternative to eliminate budgets and related gamesmanship, get the culture right, get the strategies right (adapt as needed), and require performance data to provide information that helps employees to solve problems that improve their productivity? This, too, holds promise for a large-scale reduction in bureaucratic waste.

Seventh, boards of directors need to get engaged and give top priority to the objective of experimenting and learning about how to evolve the firm to a flatter organizational structure that is attentive to the seven perspectives.

In conclusion, these seven perspectives constitute a practical approach to the improvement of organizational structure. That is, these perspectives could supply ideas to management and boards for experimenting and learning how to best organize for value creation. Also, these perspectives could suggest academic research topics tied to important practical issues.

The analysis in this chapter was guided by the Pragmatic Theory of the Firm, which views the firm as a holistic system, provides clarity about the firm's purpose, recognizes that a knowledge-building culture is the key determinant of a firm's long-term performance, and promotes systems thinking for complex issues such as organizational structure. Systems thinking is also at work in the next chapter, which describes early finance research that answers an important question: What is the most useful way to connect a firm's long-term financial performance to its market valuation?

CHAPTER 5

My Early Research at Callard, Madden & Associates

By detaching our self-image and self-worth from our beliefs, we should be more willing to stress test those beliefs instead of habitually defending them. This means that being who we are won't be tied up in maintaining a particular view, answer, opinion, or conclusion. Rather, we can define our "being" by how we think and converse. Defining everything we know as conditional [i.e., constructive skepticism]—subject to change based on new evidence—can help decouple our egos from our beliefs.[1]

—EDWARD D. HESS

The commercial research program started by Callard, Madden & Associates evolved into the HOLT (now a part of UBS) Global Database/valuation model that is used extensively by large money-management organizations. This chapter tells the story of my research in the early years of Callard, Madden & Associates that laid a foundation for connecting long-term corporate financial performance to stock market valuations.[2]

Live or Die Based on the Usefulness of Our Research

In 1970, Charles Callard and I founded Callard, Madden & Associates. Callard was an innovative economist with a passion for decoding the forecasts implied in stock prices for components of economic growth and analyzing the implications for investment portfolios. He was the first to develop a rigorous quantitative procedure to estimate an investor's discount rate (implied in stock prices) and to empirically show how inflation rates and personal tax rates impact expected returns. This work was never published. However, I summarized Callard's work in my 1999 book, *CFROI Valuation: A Total System Approach to Valuing the Firm.*[3]

Our R&D in the early years was funded by three large money-management organizations. They would continue to fund the full cost of our research program—in which we had complete control of the agenda—if, in their opinion, our research benefitted their ongoing investment performance and if our longer-term projects demonstrated practical insights that could contribute to earning above-market returns.

My focus was on corporate performance measurement and valuation. In an MBA finance course, I read an article by Merton Miller and Franco Modigliani, "Dividend Policy, Growth, and the Valuation of Shares," which laid out a valuation approach based on a firm's total assets—not the dominant return on equity (ROE) approach. Miller and Modigliani separated the firm's total value into two components: existing assets and future investments. Later, during many long days and nights at Northwestern University's computer center, I used this approach to build a "model corporation" simulation. My objective was to develop an improved measurement of accounting returns and a more useful valuation model.

My research resulted in the CFROI that is more accurate than accounting returns such as RONA or ROIC; life-cycle track records; the life-cycle valuation model that calculates the value of existing assets and the value of future investments; and the percent future metric that measures the implied value of future investments as a percentage of a firm's total market value, used for many years as a performance scorecard metric by *Barron's* and *Forbes*.

Callard and I were committed at a very early stage to using inflation-adjusted (real) discount rates, CFROIs, and reinvestment rates that drive a firm's net cash receipts (NCRs) that ultimately determine market valuations. Inflation-adjusted data is critically important to understanding the past and being better equipped to make forecasts of the future. Not adjusting for inflation leads to distortions in accounting returns that users do not fully appreciate. Inflation adjustments provide a significant benefit that is evident when studying a firm's historical track record as inflation rates vary, and for analyzing and comparing firms across countries with significantly different inflation rates. To appreciate the magnitude of the issue, Figure 5.1 plots annual inflation rates (GDP [gross domestic product] deflator) and long-term (ten-year government) interest rates.

**Figure 5.1: Annual inflation rates
and long-term interest rates, 1900–2020**

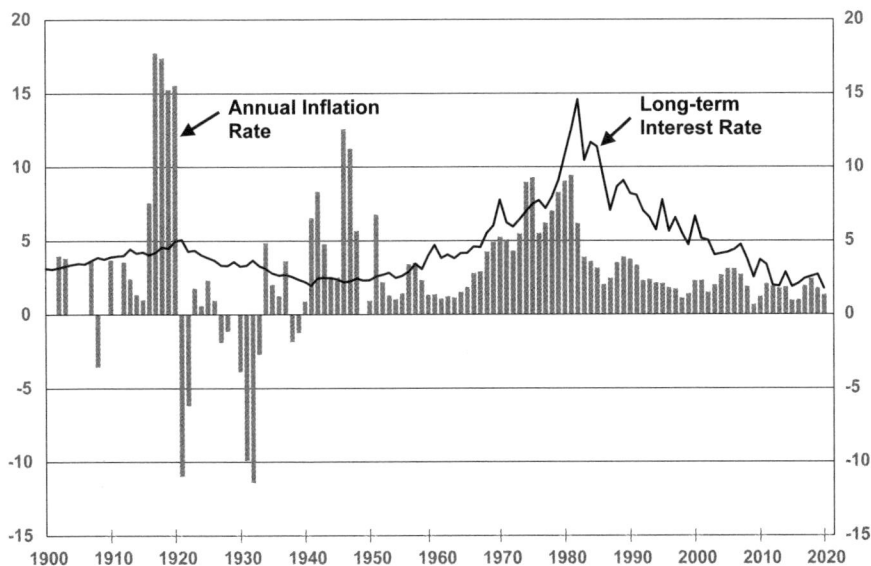

Source: GDP deflator for 1929 to 2020; earlier years use the US Bureau of Economic Analysis and CPI Index, Federal Reserve Bank of Minneapolis. Ten-year treasury rate was obtained from www.fiscaldata.treasury.gov.

Although the foundation at Callard, Madden & Associates included inflation-adjusted data, unfortunately many investors and corporate managers never gave this much thought. However, corporate performance measurement—across firms (and business units) and across historical time—gains accuracy with inflation-adjusted (real) metrics. The development of the inflation-adjusted CFROI as an improved accounting return facilitated the construction of life-cycle track records that were illustrated in chapter 1. The topic of accounting returns as estimates of economic returns (cash-out/cash-in internal rates of return) will be covered in chapter 6.

We demonstrated the importance of our commitment to inflation adjustments for our clients by using the model corporation to simulate what a typical industrial firm would report for ROE if every year its real ROI was 6 percent, which approximates the long-term cost of capital. Figure 5.2 uses a more comprehensive version (see chapter 6) of the simulation software to reproduce the early chart that was especially well received by our clients.

Figure 5.2: Simulated ROE for an industrial firm earning the cost of capital, 1900–1990

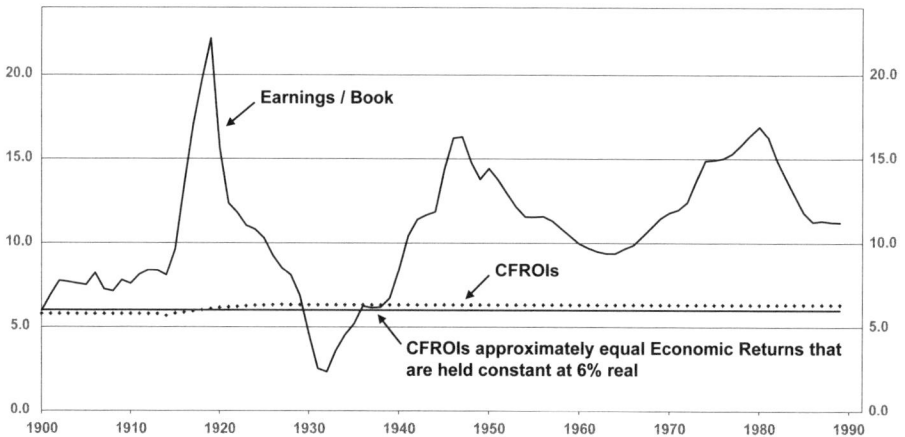

Source: Bartley J. Madden and Donn DeMuro, "Translator Simulation Software: Bridging the Gap between Accounting Returns and Economic Returns," *Journal of Applied Corporate Finance*, forthcoming 2025.

As shown in Figure 5.2, the simulated firm achieved a 6 percent real return on each year's investment. The as-reported balance sheets and income statements are simulated based on the inflation rates and interest rates shown in Figure 5.1. The inflationary and deflationary spikes during the early 1900s caused the ROE roller coaster displayed in the figure. In stark contrast, CFROIs calculated from these same financial statements approximately equal the 6 percent real returns.

The Model Corporation Simulation, Systems Thinking, and the Global Database

Callard and I shared a goal of building a first-of-its-kind global database that would be viewed as essential for decision-making in large money-management organizations. That goal necessitated systems thinking, especially for deriving the investor's discount rate used in the life-cycle valuation model, and organizing feedback to build knowledge that continually improved the accuracy and usefulness of the global database. The evolution of that global database benefitted from contributions made by many smart teammates and clients at Callard, Madden & Associates and at HOLT Value Associates, which significantly boosted its commercial acceptance. HOLT Value Associates was acquired by Credit Suisse in 2002, and the HOLT team continues the knowledge-building process. In 2023, Credit Suisse was acquired by UBS.

Writing a simulation code for our model corporation was time consuming. In the early 1970s, my Fortran program filled a box with two thousand punched cards. While this was laborious, I benefitted from having to think through all the accounting details involved with performance measurement and valuation.[4] For example, whereas finance students encounter myriad definitions of "free cash flow" used in present value calculations, we used a precise definition of NCRs to drive valuation. Figure 5.3 shows how NCRs are identical when calculated from the firm's perspective or from the capital owner's perspective.

Figure 5.3: Calculation of net cash receipts

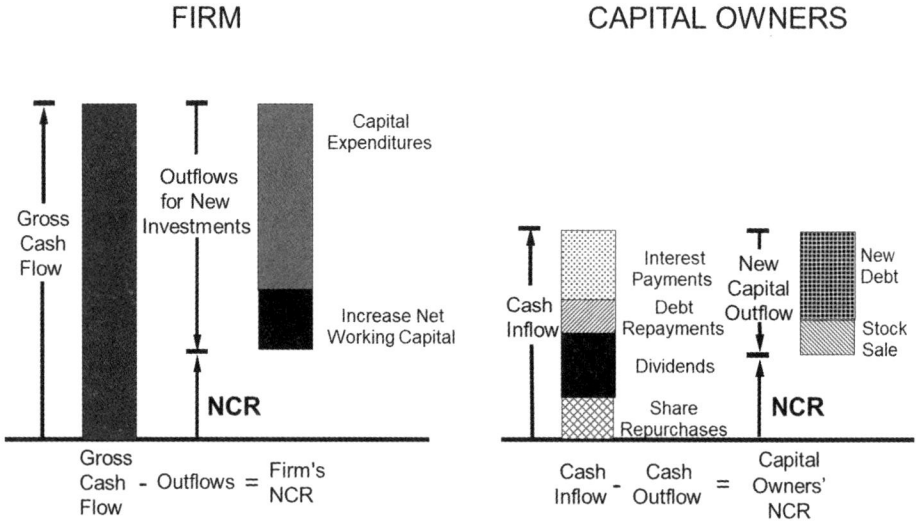

The life-cycle track record presented in Figure 5.4 provides a visual display of firm performance over time that highlights three important variables: (1) economic returns estimated by accounting returns such as CFROI, RONA, and ROIC; (2) reinvestment rates (i.e., the growth rates in resources plowed back into the business); and (3) fade rates (see chapter 1) for both economic returns and reinvestment rates.

As discussed in chapter 1, this visual display of firm performance offers insights for investors analyzing firms, for corporate managers evaluating business units and acquisition candidates, and for boards of directors responsible for approving resource allocations for the firm's business units.

Excel spreadsheets facilitate forecasting the future for these businesses and calculating valuations warranted by specific forecasts. The typical approach is to use Excel spreadsheets to calculate free cash flows (proxy for NCRs) year-by-year, and at some point, call it quits and assign a guess (estimate) about the firm's terminal value.

Figure 5.4: Life-cycle variables drive net cash receipts

LIFE-CYCLE STAGES AND MANAGEMENT PRIORITES

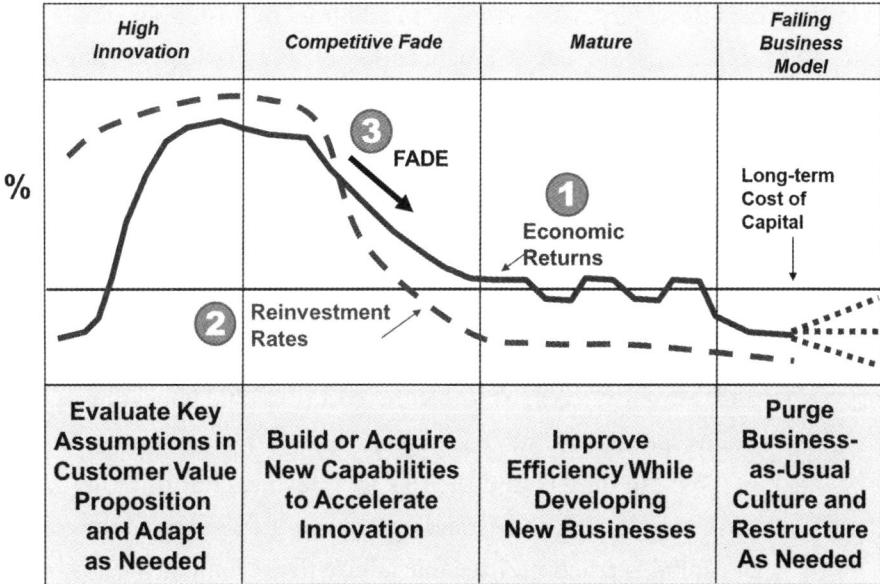

High Innovation	Competitive Fade	Mature	Failing Business Model
Evaluate Key Assumptions in Customer Value Proposition and Adapt as Needed	Build or Acquire New Capabilities to Accelerate Innovation	Improve Efficiency While Developing New Businesses	Purge Business-as-Usual Culture and Restructure As Needed

The traditional approach to valuation is not helpful to investors who want a visual guide to judge the plausibility of the forecast. If the Excel data is reconfigured to display year-by-year estimates of economic returns and reinvestment rates, then users can see the level and fade rates for these key NCR drivers. In this way, forecast life-cycle performance can be aligned with past life-cycle performance to greatly facilitate plausibility judgments.

The Investor's Discount Rate and the Life-Cycle Valuation Model

The next step is to assign a discount rate—typically referred to as the cost of capital—to discount future NCRs to a present value (i.e., a valuation warranted by the forecast). How is this cost of capital estimated? Modern finance provides the capital asset pricing model (CAPM) formula for the equity cost of capital, which is the critical input to a firm's weighted average cost of capital. CAPM's equity cost of capital is the risk-free rate plus a stock's beta times the equity risk premium, which is the expected return for the equity market in excess of the risk-free rate. This formula, however, is dysfunctional in practice due to the exceedingly wide range of estimates of the equity risk premium. In addition, estimates of beta itself can be problematic. Stephen Penman, author of several widely used textbooks on financial statement analysis and firm valuation, offers his view:

> Under the CAPM, one estimates a beta (with considerable error) then multiplies it by the "market risk premium." The latter is anyone's guess; estimates of this number in textbooks run from 3 percent to 10 percent! (Fancier asset pricing models compound the problem.) The fundamental investor must be honest in investing and, honestly, we don't know the cost of capital. Guessing at it builds speculation into a valuation.
>
> We can understand the risk in a business but thinking we can compress this understanding into one number called the cost of capital is a fiction. I see our failure to get hold of the cost of capital as the most disappointing aspect of modern finance, not that we haven't tried.[5]

As a practical matter, consider how a firm in the failing business model life-cycle stage (Figure 5.4) can have a beta of less than 1.0 and operate in a stable industry such that investors assign them lower risk than the market. Nevertheless, the plausibility of CAPM-based estimates is highly suspect for such a firm because their historical stability is expected to evaporate in the future.

Callard, Madden & Associates developed a remarkably different approach to estimate the investor's discount rate that has continued to be used by HOLT and many other investors to this day. Our task was to estimate a forward-looking discount rate that is reflected in current stock prices (or an historical point in time). The market-implied discount rate approach for stocks is also commonly used for bonds. The familiar yield to maturity is essentially the market-implied discount rate that converts an NCR stream (interest payments and principal repayment) to today's bond price. Important characteristics such as credit quality and liquidity can move a particular bond's yield to maturity above or below the average rate. This same approach is used for stocks, although the NCR stream is clearly more difficult to forecast compared to bonds.[6] However, as the forecasting procedure for a firm's NCRs improves, so does the accuracy of the company's estimated investor's discount rate. The life-cycle valuation model in Figure 5.5 shows how NCRs are generated with this approach.

Figure 5.5: Life-cycle valuation model

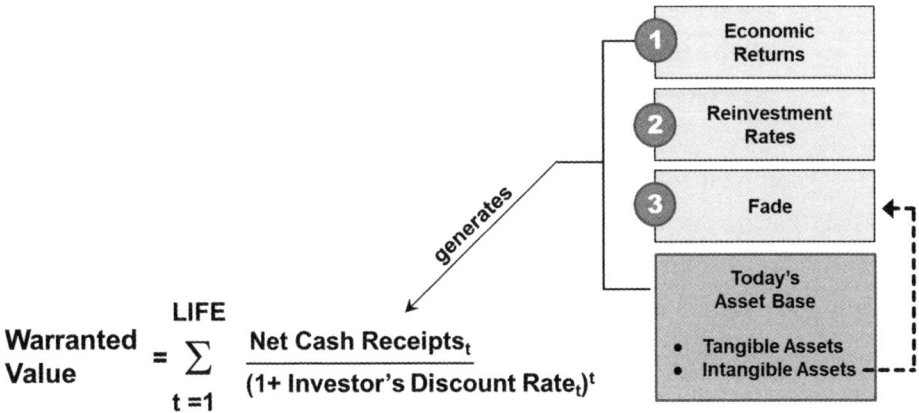

$$\text{Warranted Value} = \sum_{t=1}^{\text{LIFE}} \frac{\text{Net Cash Receipts}_t}{(1+ \text{Investor's Discount Rate}_t)^t}$$

Figure 5.5 articulates the NCR forecast via the life-cycle variables numbered 1, 2, and 3 that correspond to the variables displayed earlier in Figure 5.4. Viewing the components of the life-cycle valuation model as a system set in motion a continuous effort to improve NCR forecasts, thereby improving estimates of the investor's discount rate used in the Callard, Madden/HOLT Global Database. In contrast, the traditional valuation approach is to estimate a discount rate independent of how NCRs are forecast.

Those, like myself, who have intensely worked on improvements in the measurement of CFROIs displayed in the global database (twenty thousand firms today), have learned how smart the market is in seeing through accounting data to the actual cash flows that matter. Learning about market efficiency is a never-ending process as puzzles are presented and solutions derived for accounting adjustments to better calculate accounting returns (e.g., CFROI) to proxy for economic returns.

Both experience with life-cycle track records and empirical research confirm the following fade relationships:[7]

- The long-term tendency is for firms' CFROIs to regress toward the average economic return, which approximates the long-term cost of capital, and for reinvestment rates to regress toward an economy growth rate.
- All else equal, firms with low historical variation in CFROIs fade at a slower rate and vice versa.
- All else equal, above-average CFROIs coupled to high reinvestment rates fade faster (big opportunities attract competition).

Additional puzzles are encountered from studying warranted valuations that are calculated based on forecast fade rates using the above fade relationships. Warranted stock prices are plotted alongside historical stock prices to pinpoint sustained and significant differences between warranted (valuations) stock prices and actual stock prices. Solving these puzzles involves ongoing improvements in the measurement of assets, CFROIs, and reinvestment rates and/or improvements in forecasting fade rates for classes of firms.

Since the 1990s, intangible assets (analyzed in chapter 6) have increasingly become the source for earning above-cost-of-capital returns. This poses two new challenges for understanding accounting-based business performance: (1) capitalization and amortization of outlays for intangibles such as R&D expenditures to maintain the integrity of accounting even though published financial reports have yet to adequately address this issue, and (2) adjustments to fade forecasts (see Figure 5.5) to reflect the competitive advantage secured by intangibles. For example, platform businesses create networks that increase in value as more users join—a uniquely valuable intangible asset that generates especially favorable fade (e.g., Apple).

The key point is that a process of continually improving NCR forecasts means that, on average, these forecasts are getting closer to the actual

NCRs that will be delivered by firms in the future. Hence, calculations of the investor's discount rates will become more useful for investors.

Life-cycle track records and the life-cycle valuation model enable users to continually learn about how firms create/dissipate value over the long term and how the stock market reflects that change in value. An insightful understanding of what drives stock prices can incentivize management and the board to invest for the long term and not be enamored with Wall Street's hyperfocus on quarterly earnings. Importantly, this life-cycle framework provides investors with a toolbox for analyzing a firm's history and developing plausible scenarios for likely long-term future fade rates that should be compared to expectations implied in the current stock price. Students would benefit greatly if business schools provide this life-cycle framework as an integral part of a student's education.

Excess (Positive/Negative) Shareholder Returns

The utility of implementing the life-cycle framework discussed in this chapter is particularly evident in explaining long-term moves in stock prices that produce significant excess (positive/negative) shareholder returns. For example, let's examine month-end prices for Walmart 1980–2000 (see Figure 5.6). Note that Walmart outperformed the S&P 500 thirteenfold over the ten-year period 1980–1990.

Investigating the causes of excess shareholder returns over the long term requires quantification of investor expectations of financial performance at the beginning of the period and comparison to subsequent financial performance. The life-cycle framework is ideally suited for his task.

Figure 5.6: Walmart stock prices, 1980–2000

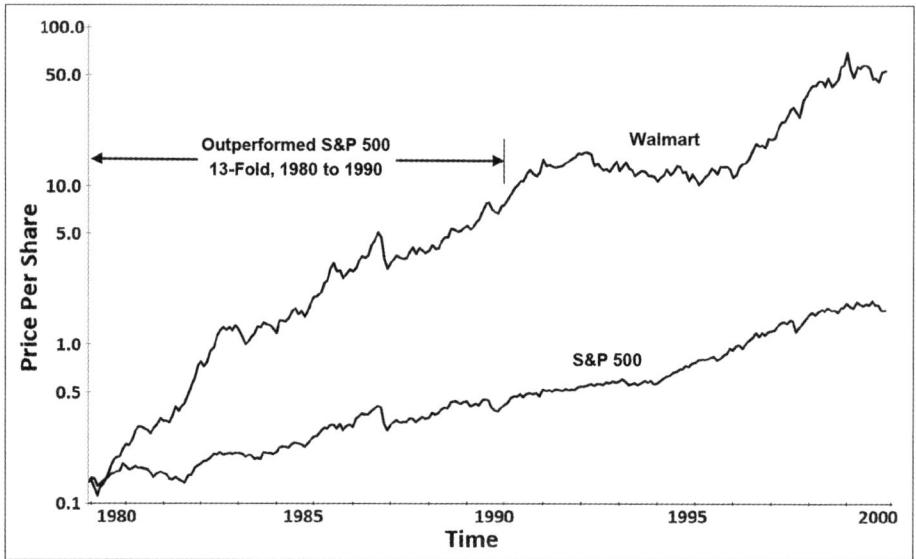

At the beginning of the period, given the known market value of the firm and the estimated investor discount rate, we use the life-cycle valuation model to derive the implied future NCR stream. Deviations of the expected life-cycle performance from the actual determine excess shareholder returns.

Importantly, professional money managers who utilize the life-cycle framework routinely quantify investor expectations of future fade rates. In seeking excess (positive) shareholder returns, they use the term "beat the fade" for the possibility that a firm will generate a future fade rate that is more favorable than current market expectations.

With a known market value for Walmart and an estimated investor's discount rate at year-end 1979, the implied future life-cycle fades were calculated using the life-cycle valuation model. In a sense, we run the valuation model in reverse. Instead of calculating a warranted value based on forecasted fade rates for CFROIs and asset growth rates, we derive implied future fade rates. Figure 5.7 summarizes.

**Figure 5.7: Walmart investor expectations
calculated at year end, 1979 (dashed lines)**

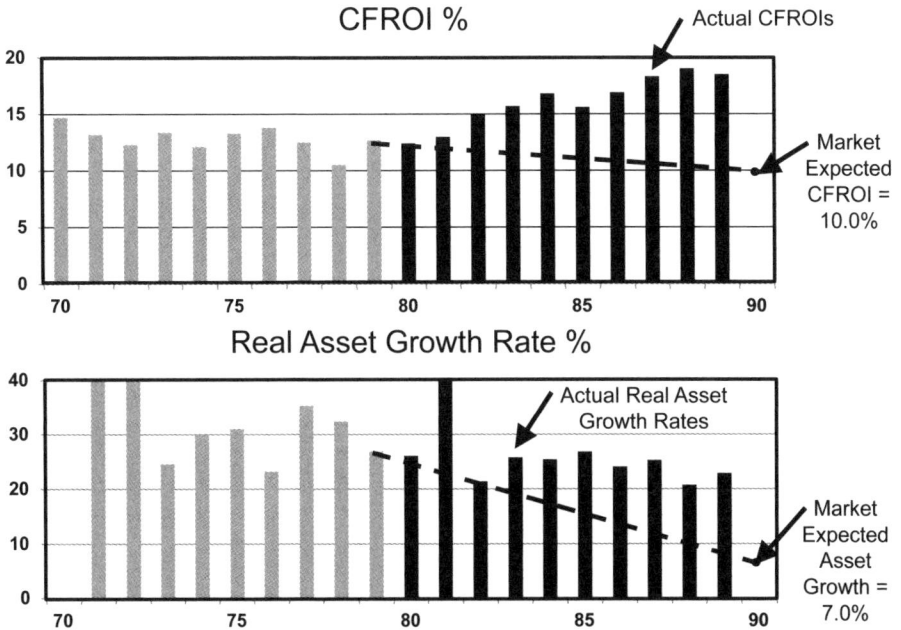

Source: HOLT Global Database

As shown in Figure 5.7, from 1970 to 1980, Walmart achieved real CFROIs of 13 percent, substantially greater than the 6 percent real long-term cost of capital. Real asset growth rates (reinvestment rates) were approximately 30 percent—an astonishingly high number for a large firm. Using Walmart's stock price at year-end 1979 and HOLT's estimated discount rate, we calculated (see Figure 5.5) market expectations for CFROIs to regress to 10 percent in ten years and real asset growth rates to regress to 7 percent.

Walmart delivered an upward fade of CFROIs (shown as black bars), and substantially exceeded the expected CFROI fade to 10 percent. Moreover, its real asset growth rates (black bars) greatly exceeded the expected fade to 7 percent. This explains, visually and intuitively, why Walmart outperformed the S&P 500 thirteenfold over this time period.

In conclusion, the commercial research program that started in 1970 kept me grounded in searching for deeper understanding of the causes that resulted in life-cycle track records and related stock price histories. That search generated new insights regarding value creation by firms, which led me to develop the Pragmatic Theory of the Firm.

Connecting a firm's financial performance to its market valuation requires the minimizing of distortions in accounting returns due to not adequately handling intangible assets, which is the topic of the next chapter.

CHAPTER 6

It's Time for the New Economy Accounting

In times of change learners inherit the earth, while the learned find themselves beautifully equipped to deal with a world that no longer exists.

—ERIC HOFFER[1]

Generally accepted accounting principles (GAAP) represent efforts by accounting rule makers to shape the form and content of the financial statements. GAAP, however, also shapes the worldview of accounting rule makers and, in turn, determines how they perceive accounting challenges. The Financial Accounting Standards Board (FASB), the leading accounting rule-making body overseeing financial reporting, has assessed the accounting challenges due to the New Economy and concluded: (1) the FASB's purpose is to assist existing and potential investors and lenders with decisions about providing resources to the firm, and (2) regardless of claims that the New Economy has made GAAP obsolete, the status quo still offers the most efficient way for FASB to achieve its purpose.[2] This has led accounting scholars to conclude that "the enormous resources and attention devoted to written rules have been accompanied by waning professional responsibility for good judgment and regard for practice and practicality."[3]

This chapter explains how intangible assets (ignored by GAAP) have fueled the growth of the New Economy. We then utilize the Pragmatic Theory of the Firm to contrast the firm's purpose with the FASB's purpose. Next, we propose a practical first step in the evolution of the New Economy accounting by improving the accounting return metrics used by management to measure business unit performance. The final section explains how accounting returns get distorted and then reviews simulation software (open access) to offer those in the trenches a learning tool for incorporating intangibles to improve accounting return metrics. The advances we propose should be of interest to managers wanting to create value in the firm, along with a financial statement for users wanting to measure value creation for investment decisions.

The New Economy

The hallmark of value creation in the Old Economy was mass production facilitated by tangible assets (e.g., plant and equipment, inventory, physical stores, etc.). Gaining a customer yielded an incremental benefit. However, New Economy firms, like Facebook, eBay, LinkedIn, etc., operate platform businesses in which the value of their network increases for all users as more users join. In the New Economy, therefore, tangible assets are commodities that typically are easily obtained and, by themselves, are rarely the source of greater-than-cost-of-capital investment returns.

The New Economy is a fast-paced world of change in which rapid knowledge building and adaptation are essential for sustaining competitive advantage. Employees' human capital, nurtured and expanded by a firm's culture keyed to knowledge-building proficiency, is the root cause of intangible assets ignored by today's Old Economy accounting. Consider how researchers, software engineers, and marketing personnel who orchestrate advertising campaigns spend resources to produce valuable patents, innovative new products, platforms, and desirable brand names. Yet these outlays are neither capitalized on the balance sheet nor subsequently amortized. Rather, they are buried in the income statement's selling, general, and administrative (SG&A) expenses.

Imagine that you are the head accountant for a firm and aware of what is behind the numbers in reported SG&A expenses. You, and not users of the firm's accounting reports, are aware of expenditures that qualify as contributing to benefits beyond the annual accounting period (i.e., capital assets). These may include outlays for employee (knowledge-building) training, big-data analytics and AI software, ecosystem/platform development, process improvements, R&D, advertising, and expenditures for the net-zero transition. This source of long-term value creation and competitive advantage is hidden from users of accounting reports.[4]

Here is a way to think about capital (balance sheet) assets. Capital assets are embedded ideas.[5] The New Economy is about ideas that produce, for the most part, nonphysical things (i.e., intangible assets), whereas the Old Economy is about ideas that primarily produced physical things like pumps and electrical switches.

Oil reserves, for example, greatly increased in value after new ideas produced the internal combustion engine. It is straightforward to visualize depreciation schedules (accounting lives) for pumps, switches, and oil reserves. This is not so easy for intangible assets. For example, it is straightforward to estimate depreciation expenses for Amazon's physical stores but not so easy for their core platform that more efficiently enables customers to get what they want at lower cost versus Old Economy stores. But that does not justify maintaining the status quo ostensibly to protect the objectivity and reliability of balance sheet asset figures.

AI will generate disruptive value creation ideas that spawn an explosion in intangible assets, further accelerating the obsolescence of the Old Economy accounting system. The result will be misleading earnings and accounting returns on capital with increased potential for poor decision-making and misallocation of resources.

In their impactful article, "Evolution in Value Relevance of Accounting Information," Mary Barth, Ken Li, and Charles McClure note:

> Prior research finds that value relevance of accounting items, particularly earnings, has declined, [while attributing] the decline to the rise of this New Economy, and concludes that accounting has

> lost its relevance. We consider a larger set of accounting items . . .
> which are important in the new economy. We find increases in
> value relevance of these items offset earnings' decline. . . . Finding
> increased value relevance of items relating to intangible assets,
> growth opportunities, and alternative performance measures—
> despite their incomplete reflection in accounting—reveals that
> this information is relevant to investors in the New Economy.[6]

The Pragmatic Theory of the Firm Clarifies Purpose

A growing body of research has argued for the capitalization and amortization of intangibles to improve the usability of the balance sheet and income
statement.[7] Stock prices are frequently used to proxy for how investors
react to accounting data contained in quarterly and annual reports.

An alternative view is to ask, what is the purpose of the firm? That is a
productive beginning point for proposing a first step for the New Economy
accounting. Moreover, the Pragmatic Theory of the Firm provides a holistic
view of the firm and specifies its four-part purpose. A critical component
of which (especially relevant for equity and debt owners) is to survive and
prosper over the long term. Nothing works long-term if the firm steadfastly
fails to earn the cost of capital. As discussed in chapter 1, the life-cycle
track records are the foundational performance scorecard consistent with
the firm's long-term objective to survive and prosper.

Life-cycle track records consist of time series of economic returns
(estimated via accounting returns on capital expressed as RONA, ROIC,
CFROI, etc.) versus the cost of capital and of reinvestment rates.[8] Not
only is this a bare minimum of data, but the data already exists, although
without adjustments for intangibles. A strong case can be made that boards
of directors should require historical life-cycle track records with forecasts for each of the firm's business units as an integral part of any major
resource allocation decision.

There is a subtle yet important difference between the stated purpose
of the FASB that focuses on the needs of *outside* capital owners versus
the purpose of the firm that compels management and boards to make

resource allocation (*inside* the firm) decisions that create long-term value. The latter purpose spotlights the need to reduce distortions in life-cycle track records (and related economic profit displays) caused by not properly including intangible assets. From society's perspective, the potential benefit is substantial. We are proposing a method for improving resource allocation decisions exactly where improvements matter most.

As an aside, in 2001, I was involved with making the first major intangibles-related improvement to the HOLT Global Database used by money-management organizations worldwide, which is the data source for the life-cycle track records discussed in this book. This first step was to estimate accounting lives for a firm's R&D expenditures to enable capitalization and amortization, thereby improving the levels and trends of both CFROIs and reinvestment rates displayed as life-cycle track records.[9] These track records are a critical part of HOLT clients' analysis of firms to make buy/hold/sell investment decisions. These clients are smart, hard-nosed portfolio managers and security analysts, and their decisions impact portfolio performance, which in turn impacts their compensation (and job security). The intangibles-related improvements were enthusiastically received by this tough-to-please crowd. We can expect a similar reaction from management and boards when they experience the before versus the after return metrics.

Successful implementation of the initial steps requires a commitment from management. Consider Baruch Lev's opinion about the apparent failure of management to pressure the accounting rule makers for change:

> My sense is that executives' opposition to intangibles' capitalization reflects their reluctance to present on the balance assets (capitalization intangibles) whose value can be impaired, or even vanish when disrupted by new technologies. Investors' consequent questions about why the intangibles were not properly protected against disruption, or even why the investments were made in the first place will surely be embarrassing. Better, from managers' perspective, to expense all intangibles immediately, thereby leaving no trace of them in the financial reports.[10]

The next section presents a practical approach for a major step forward in the evolution of the New Economy accounting.

Management Development of an Intangibles Accounting Database

The first step is to provide useful intangibles data to management. However, we have not ignored the problem of incorporating intangibles as part of a major upgrade of GAAP to benefit outside investors. Our strategy has two steps. Step one: The firm should build up much needed experiences (knowledge base) from estimating accounting lives for intangibles, improve life-cycle track records for business units, and make better resource allocation decisions. Success with step one should reduce FASB's uncertainty for taking step two: adjust for intangibles in accounting reports used by investors. Note that acquired intangibles (e.g., R&D, brands) are currently recorded on the acquiror's balance sheet because FASB views these data as "objectively" tied to a market price. Useful estimates for internally generated intangibles are certainly doable.[11]

The crux of step one is the construction of an intangibles accounting database (IAD)—perhaps a task delegated to CFOs and their staffs. The IAD should contain data on selected variables from SG&A. The key data are estimated accounting lives for these intangible assets. Figure 6 illustrates the game plan for the IAD.

As shown in Figure 6.1, the combination of GAAP data with IAD data enables management and the board to work with much improved life-cycle track records, thereby leading to better value creation decisions. We would expect management to improve their communications with investors by providing highlights of important IAD variables, especially so for sophisticated money-management firms that construct their own track record displays from publicly available accounting reports. Those investors would be highly appreciative of IAD-derived insights that lead to more informed investment decisions.

Figure 6.1: Firm's Intangibles Accounting Database

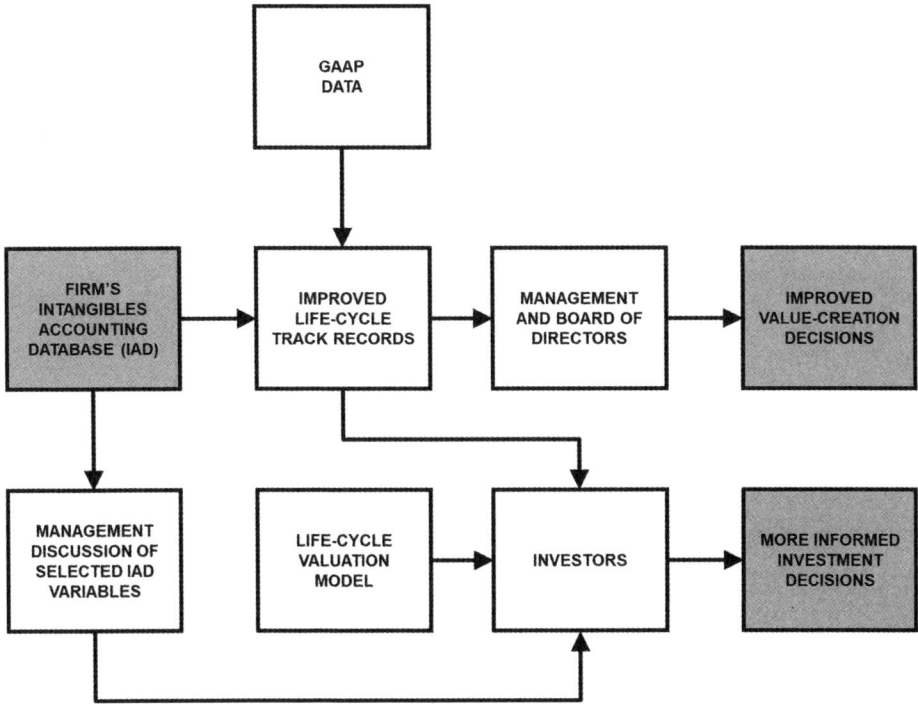

Source: Bartley J. Madden and Douglas E. Stevens, "Increasing the Value of Accounting for Management, Boards, and Investors: A Path Forward for the New Economy," SSRN working paper (2024).

Accounting returns play the central role in life-cycle track records and resource allocations. It is therefore important to understand what causes distortions in these returns.

How Accounting Returns Are Distorted

An economic return has a precise definition. For an investment with known cash outlays and cash receipts over its investment life, the economic return is the internal rate of return (IRR). However, an accounting return is a snapshot in time derived from accounting statements that average ongoing investments initiated over previous years, each with potentially different economic returns over time.

Figure 6.2 summarizes key points about accounting return metrics most often encountered in practice and in the academic literature.

Figure 6.2: Comparison of accounting returns

Accounting Return	Definition	Comments
ROE Return-On-Equity	$\dfrac{\text{Net Income}}{\text{Common Equity}}$	Increasing debt can boost earnings/book but increase variability and related risk.
RONA Return-On-Net-Assets	$\dfrac{\text{Net Income + Interest}}{\text{Net Assets}}$	RONA and ROIC have similar calculations. When assets age, their net value declines thereby boosting RONA. Old facilities especially exhibit a much biased (higher) RONA.
CRR Cash Recovery Rate	$\dfrac{\text{Cash Flow}}{\text{Gross Assets}}$	CRR is the rate of getting cash back relative to what was invested. Importantly, it is not an internal rate of return (IRR).
CFROI Cash-Flow-Return-On-Investment	IRR calculation uses gross assets, proportion nondepreciating assets, cash flow, and accounting life plus inflation adjustments	Inputs of key variables add complexity as do inflation adjustments. Benefits include increased accuracy and comparability across historical time periods with different inflation environments. The use of gross assets avoids the RONA asset age bias.

Security analysts rely on two workhorse accounting return metrics:

- RONA is calculated with published financial statement data as shown above. Variations of RONA include the use of NOPAT (net operating profit after tax). Minor variations are frequently labeled ROIC.
- The other workhorse metric is a leveraged return (i.e., ROE, see chapter 5, Figure 5.2).

Less frequently encountered are cash recovery rate (CRR) and CFROI. Note the intuitive appeal of CRR: the rate of getting cash back versus the cash given up. While the simplicity of CRR is certainly appealing for business unit applications, care is needed since CRR is not an IRR (as is CFROI) and not directly comparable to a cost of capital.

The key issues involved with adjusting RONA to compensate for the omission of intangibles are:

- Net income in the numerator of the RONA calculation increases because the full outlay for intangibles in SG&A expenditures is replaced with a smaller deduction for amortization of intangibles. RONA increases due to the numerator increasing.
- Net assets in the denominator increase due to net intangibles being added to the net asset base. RONA decreases due to the denominator increasing.
- Complex impacts on RONA result from different accounting lives for intangibles and different reinvestment (organic) growth rates.

The Academic History of Accounting Returns

Let's briefly highlight the history of academic research on the topic of accounting returns versus economic returns.[12]

From the mid-1960s to the mid-1980s, a substantial number of journal articles demonstrated that accounting returns differ significantly from economic returns. Academic interest in this line of research was encouraged by Geoffrey Harcourt's 1965 article, "The Accountant in a Golden Age." Harcourt introduced investments having different patterns of cash receipts over time and noted the challenge of capturing economic returns with traditional accounting returns:

> It had been hoped that some rough "rules of thumb" might be developed; and that these would allow accounting rates of profit to be adjusted for the lengths of life of machines, the patterns of quasi-rents, rates of growth, and the method of depreciation used. However, it is obvious from the calculations that the relationships are too complicated to allow this.[13]

The above conclusion was echoed in a highly cited 1983 article by Franklin Fischer and John McGowan:

> There is no way in which one can look at accounting rates of return and infer anything about relative economic profitability. . . . The economic rate of return is difficult—perhaps impossible—to compute for entire firms. Doing so requires information about both the past and the future which outside observers do not have, if it exists at all.[14]

The pessimism of these researchers permeates Richard Brief's book (1986), a compilation of the most influential articles on accounting returns versus economic returns.[15] One such article by Thomas Stauffer documented, for a wide variety of conditions, the magnitude and sign of deviations from true economic returns for both RONA and CRR.[16]

Yuji Ijiri offered an approach to infer economic returns by avoiding, as a starting point, the accounting return with its reliance on earnings. Instead, he began with the CRR:

> A corporation invests in a variety of projects, each having a different cash recovery pattern (including a different economic life). However, if it is reasonable to assume that a mix of such projects as well as the cash flow patterns of these projects are reasonably stable over time, then corporate investments may be regarded as repeated investments in a given composite project with a given cash flow pattern over its life.
>
> Earnings are, however, directly affected by depreciation and other noncash charges and credits, which are subject to many discretionary judgments of the corporation. . . . The recovery-rate approach is, on the other hand, strictly based on cash flows which are more objective and less subject to arbitrary discretions of the corporation than earnings.[17]

Gerald Salamon built mathematical models to derive the IRR implications from variation in the CRR life and the time patterns of cash receipts over a specified life. Andrew Stark compiled Salamon's work and other similarly impactful articles into his 1990 book.[18]

William Baber and Sok-Hyon Kand extended the CRR approach

with their 1996 study of the US pharmaceutical industry.[19] Based on a variety of assumptions of time patterns of cash receipts, investment life, and growth rates for invested capital, the authors conducted a sensitivity analysis of accounting returns, CRRs, and estimated IRRs that showed improved estimates of IRRs using cash flows. Building on their work, Shivaram Rajgopal, Anup Srivastava, and Rong Zhao, in a 2023 article in the *Accounting Review*, sharpened the estimating process for IRRs including adjustments for intangibles. The authors noted:

> Nevertheless, critics remain uncomfortable with IRR because it is based on several assumptions about the length and time distribution of benefits generated by investments and the growth rate of investments . . . Yet critics ignore that ARRs [accounting rates of return] rely on an even greater number of assumptions, including the capitalization or expensing of investment outlays (physical versus intangibles, acquired versus self-developed), revenue recognition, conservative accounting such as impairments and restructuring charges, and depreciation policy. The only difference is that a researcher makes the assumptions in calculating IRRs, while ARRs are based on accounting numbers derived from numerous conventions and managers' assumptions.[20]

Accounting returns such as RONA differ in complex ways from the cash-out/cash-in real (inflation-adjusted) economic returns. In particular, the upsurge in intangible investments since the 1990s has resulted in major ongoing distortions to RONA.

CFOs and their staffs would benefit from the ability to analyze the effects on RONA due to alternative capitalization and amortization schedules for specific intangible assets.[21] Consequently, I partnered with Donn DeMuro, a software expert and a former colleague who wrote foundational code for the global databases of Callard, Madden & Associates and HOLT. We coauthored a paper analyzing intangibles and accounting returns that also explains the learning benefits from the Translator simulation software (open access), which is highlighted in Figure 6.3.[22]

Figure 6.3: The Translator simulation software facilitates learning

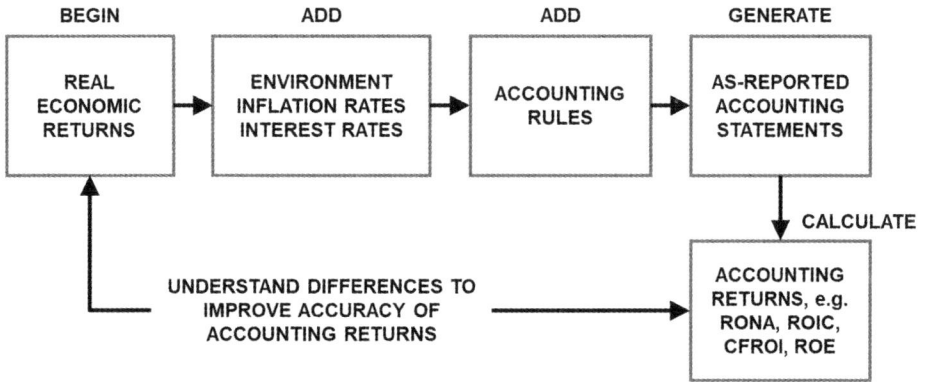

Figure 6.3 diagrams a learning process well suited for management (guided by CFOs) to finally address distorted performance measurements across their business units. This is especially important for high-intensity intangibles businesses and businesses operating in environments with much higher inflation rates than the US (e.g., Brazil, Argentina).

Figure 6.4 illustrates the running of the Translator simulation software. The environment selected was the actual US inflation rates and interest rates from 1990 to 2020 (see chapter 5, Figure 5.1). The asset configuration inputted reflects a typical industrial firm with tangible assets equal to intangible assets.[23] The foundational variables that drive the simulation are the life-cycle inputs—time series of real (inflation-adjusted) economic returns and real reinvestment rates shown at the bottom of Figure 6.4. As-reported (consistent with the specified environment) balance sheets and income statements were generated that, in turn, were used to calculate period-by-period accounting returns. For example, the unadjusted RONA is plotted as the top line. The RONA intangibles-adjusted is lower and closer to the economic returns. Finally, RONA intangibles-adjusted was derived for a zero-inflation environment and closely tracks the economic returns. This type of analysis can identify the magnitude of accounting return distortions for each of the firm's business units based on their asset configurations and reinvestment rates.

**Figure 6.4: Impacts of adjustments to RONA
for a specific environment and asset configuration**

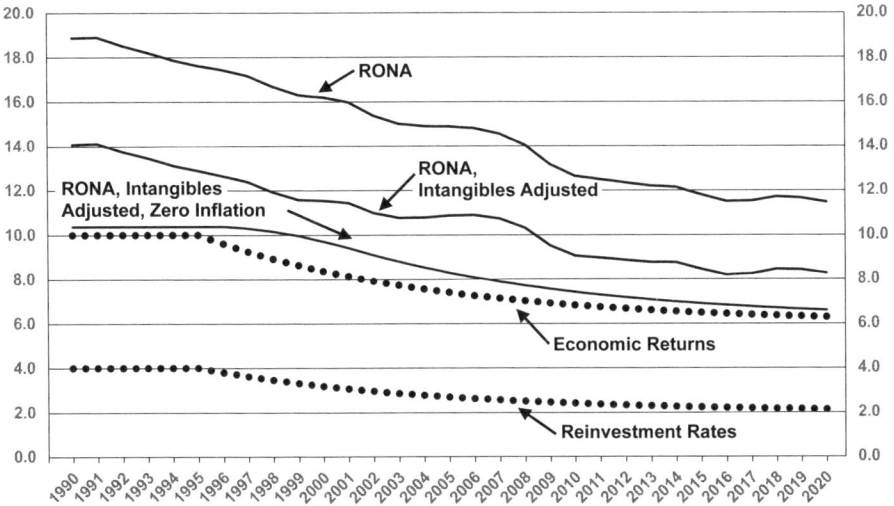

Source: Bartley J. Madden and Donn DeMuro, "Translator Simulation Software: Bridging the Gap between Accounting Returns and Economic Returns," *Journal of Applied Corporate Finance*, forthcoming 2025.

In conclusion, a major step forward for the New Economy accounting is for management to address the distortions in the accounting returns across their portfolio of business units by implementing an IAD. A plausible scenario is that, over time, industry best practices evolve for estimating accounting lives for intangible assets. This would lead to improved accounting returns and life-cycle-type performance displays, thereby improving internal decision-making. This bottom-up demonstration of the practical use of intangibles accounting should expedite change by the FASB to benefit external users of GAAP-based financial statements.

CHAPTER 7

Free to Choose Medicine

The single most powerful explanation for how the FDA works is . . . the bureaucratic imperative that seeks to expand turf no matter what its consequences to others.[1]

—RICHARD A. EPSTEIN

In 2003 I took early retirement to begin a new hybrid academic career: writing journal articles, monographs, and books on a wide variety of topics broadly dealing with value creation and systems thinking. A major feature of my work has been the application of a systems thinking lens regardless of the topic analyzed.

An early project I developed was to apply value creation and systems thinking to the FDA's drug and medical treatment approval process. That project resulted in my Free to Choose Medicine (FTCM) proposal to enable patients and their doctors to access innovative, not-yet-FDA-approved drugs (medical treatments in general) that have demonstrated initial safety and efficacy—most importantly, new treatments that target life-threatening diseases. I have found that a systems view of the FDA provides valuable insights, including the foundational purpose of the FDA regulatory system.

The second Trump administration is expected to address the excessive cost (time and money) for drug developers to obtain FDA approvals. Also, the Promising Pathway Act (PPA) should be reintroduced in Congress in 2025 and would implement FTCM principles for rare, life-threatening diseases. FDA reform is likely to gain bipartisan support for the reasons explained in this chapter.

Systems Thinking and the FDA

In 1962, federal legislation expanded the FDA monopoly to evaluate and decide what new therapeutic drugs should be approved for marketing in the United States. As a result, the FDA's goal became to ensure that approved drugs are *safe and effective.* Randomized control trials (RCTs) became the gold standard for clinical testing.

More than six decades later, we are burdened by sky-high prescription drug prices largely due to the FDA's continued demands for ever more expensive (time and money) clinical trials.[2] Although we are experiencing an extraordinarily rapid rate of medical science innovation, unfortunately the most innovative new drugs are moving at a snail's pace via testing that is rooted in legislation developed in a technology environment far different from that of today. Technology in 1962 was primitive compared to today's high-speed personal computers, internet, and powerful AI-driven big-data analytics applied to "real world" (not RCT) data. Couple this with patients' genetic data and drug biomarkers, and instead of crude effectiveness based on the average patient, groups of patients can be quantified and studied for treatment results and adverse side effects. The FDA's regulatory process is antiquated due to its focus on statistically significant results for the average patient in late-stage clinical trials.

Patients in such trials have considerable variation in genetics and biochemistry and treatment results. After the completed trials, a drug could have demonstrated highly effective outcomes for one group of patients but not so for another group. As explained in this chapter, FTCM accommodates (exploits) this situation. However, the FDA's focus on the average patient can incentivize drug developers to strive for adequate, perhaps mediocre, treatment results so as to reduce the risk of not getting FDA approval.

Not surprisingly, it can easily take a biopharmaceutical firm a dozen years to complete clinical testing and FDA review. However, as the pace of medical knowledge building increases, the FDA's excessive caution comes at a steep cost. While the news media reports in detail unexpected deaths from approved drugs, not reported is the invisible graveyard filled by those who were, are, and will be denied access to new lifesaving drugs.

The FDA's focus on safety and effectiveness is often accepted without questioning its costs. "Safe" and "effective" are relative terms that necessarily involve patients with their unique health conditions and risk/reward preferences. Further, these terms imply important tradeoffs using information that is known to doctors and patients but not to the FDA. Elazer Edelman summarizes the magnitude of this problem:

> As long as society is informed that risk and benefit travel together, and is made aware of their relative weights, then society can decide how to balance these two elements. The failure to inform, the lack of understanding and the inability to recognize that there is this balance is the biggest problem.[3]

A practical means to "balance these two elements" is detailed in a later section of this chapter that describes the Free to Choose Medicine proposal. But first, in the spirit of systems thinking and knowledge building promoted throughout this book, let's analyze the FDA's regulatory process as part of a larger system. Taking a societal perspective, a purpose for the FDA that will benefit society, especially patients, is to deliver *better drugs, sooner, at lower cost.*

Rarely acknowledged is that the FDA's prolonged clinical requirements also impact the "better drugs" objective, and this needs explanation. This occurs in an environment of unprecedented speed in knowledge building about human biology manifested in gene therapies, personalized vaccines, enhanced human-relevant models of disease (organ-on-a-chip technologies), and AI-enabled drug discovery and development. This knowledge building can potentially expedite the delivery of better drugs for FDA clinical testing. But to realize this potential, it is in society's interest for venture capital to readily fund startup biopharmaceutical firms with top scientific talent focused on breakthrough medical treatments (including cures) for our most serious health issues where the standard of care (FDA-approved treatments) has limited efficacy. Dr. John Freund, a noted venture capitalist, explains the negative impacts of the FDA's long and costly approval process on external funding:

> I run a venture capital firm specializing in pharmaceutical drug and medical device companies. Those of us on the front lines, who see innovative health-care companies from the inside in a way the FDA does not, see the negative impacts of the FDA's approval process first hand on a daily basis.
>
> Several years ago, for example, the FDA tightened up the requirements for approving new drugs for adult-onset diabetes, a disease that affects approximately 25 million Americans. The result is that performing the clinical trials for a new diabetes drug is so long and costly that no venture capital firm will finance a new diabetes drug. . . .
>
> The FDA tightened the requirements to get new antibiotics approved, and the result will be that fewer drugs to treat deadly resistant bacteria will be developed in the future.[4]

Given the FDA status quo, drug development firms with limited capital may have a multitude of potential breakthroughs but necessarily must bet the farm on one candidate. Radically different breakthrough drugs are often shelved because their mechanism of action substantially differs from mainstream drugs; and the FDA's excessive caution means exceedingly difficult (and hard to forecast) late-stage clinical trial endpoints.

Sam Kazman aptly describes the culture at the FDA:

> From FDA commissioner to the bureau heads to the individual NDA [new drug approval] reviewers, the message is clear: if you approve a drug with unanticipated side effects, both you and the agency will face the heat of newspaper headlines, television

coverage and congressional hearings. On the other hand, if FDA insists on more and more data from a manufacturer, and finally approves a drug, which should have been on the market . . . years before, there is no such price to pay.

Drug lag's victims and their families will hardly be complaining, because they won't know what hit them. . . . They only know that there is nothing their doctors can do for them. From the standpoint of . . . politics, they are invisible.[5]

The entire FDA testing and approval process is clearly not operated to produce better drugs, sooner, at lower cost for the benefit of existing and future patients. Rather, it is designed to make it easier for the FDA to make and defend its drug approval decisions. It believes that long delays are necessary for adequate scientific testing.

Are we better off with the status quo FDA? Mary Ruwart in her book, *Death by Regulation,* provides an especially rigorous and comprehensive analysis. Ruwart, with a PhD in biophysics, spent two decades as a pharmaceutical research scientist for Upjohn (owned by Pfizer). She also has in-depth knowledge of the academic literature. Here is her short answer to our question:

The [1962 FDA legislation] amendments may have saved us from the 10% of ineffective drugs that were on the market, but at what cost? Clearly, today's drugs have been made much more expensive—perhaps as much as 40 times what they otherwise would have been—because of the tripling of development time and exponential increases in the costs of studies necessary for approval. The [late-stage clinical trials] effectiveness studies are one of the most-expensive regulatory requirements and cost consumers many times more than the waste that they supposedly prevent. . . .

Even if some of the estimates used to make those calculations are off by a factor of 100, the conclusion—that the Amendments' side effects outweigh their benefits—will not change.[6]

There is little doubt that lengthier trials with more patients can generate more statistically robust results; but again, at what cost? The plight of today's patients who are denied access to innovative drugs is FDA rationalized as the necessary price to benefit future patients. This is a simple enough argument for a monopolist to make. In the competitive private sector, a company would not survive if it cared so little for its current customers. Ask yourself if today's capabilities of cell phones would exist if the AT&T monopolistic control of the US communications infrastructure was not dismantled.

Competition Benefits Patients and the FDA's Regulatory Efficiency

In answer to patients demanding freedom to make informed decisions as to early access to promising new drugs, the FDA asserts that it is providing needed consumer protection. Translation: You and I (advised by our doctors) are not smart enough to make our own health decisions (attuned to our unique health conditions and risk preferences) regarding not-yet-approved drugs.

A strong case can be made that with today's technology, the path forward should be Free to Choose Medicine. Importantly, FTCM is a competitive alternative and not a replacement for the FDA regulatory process. Figure 7.1 illustrates how FTCM would work.[7]

Figure 7.1 details the FDA's regulatory process with Phase I clinical trials evaluating safety and Phase II RCTs evaluating both safety and efficacy. Phase III involves expanded RCTs, and Phase III success leads to FDA review. The statistical power of RCTs depends on a homogeneous subset of patients with one group receiving the drug being tested and the other receiving either a placebo or a standard-of-care treatment. When the majority of doctors feel strongly that the new drug is superior to the standard of care, a troubling moral issue is raised. Patients fighting a serious or even life-threatening disease who do not receive the new drug are left with the platitude that their participation in the trial will benefit future patients.

Figure 7.1: Core components of Free to Choose Medicine

FREE TO CHOOSE MEDICINE

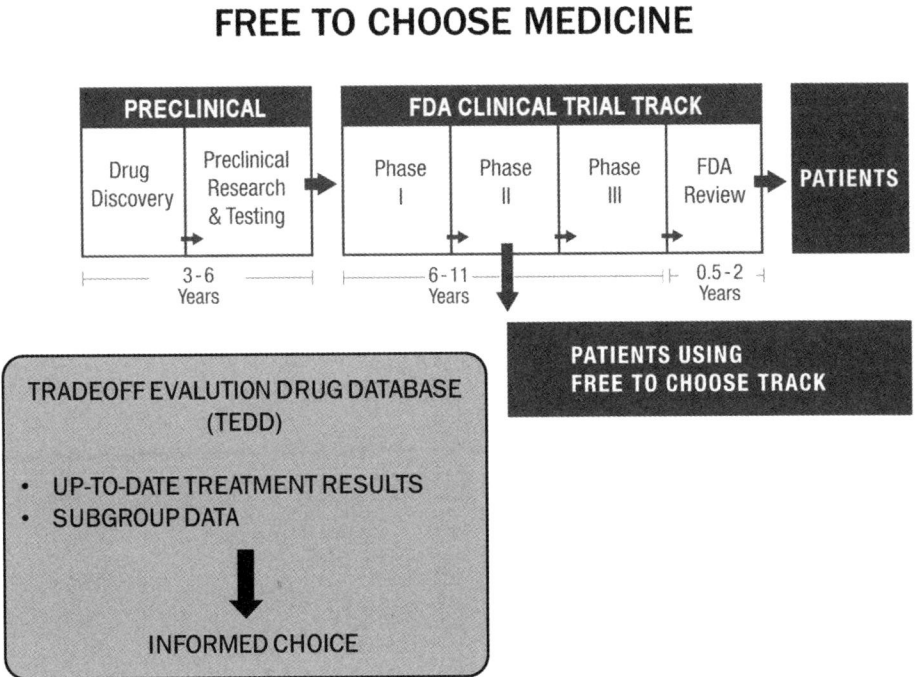

But medical innovation is progressing at such a rapid pace that RCTs will be ill-suited to evaluate a "sample of one" (i.e., customized drugs/ vaccines uniquely attuned to the patient's genetics/biomarkers such that the risk of adverse side effects is minimal and common sense argues to expedite access).

Returning to Figure 7.1, FTCM legislation would enable a committee to evaluate a request from a drug developer to participate on the FTCM track and receive provisional approval. That evaluation would be based on safety and efficacy demonstrated from successfully completing Phase I and at least one Phase II trial. Continued participation on the FTCM track would depend upon the committee concluding that up-to-date treatment results are consistent with patient benefits. Sustained and significant beneficial- to-patients treatment results could lead to the FDA granting full approval.

These real-world treatment results (data) would be housed in a Tradeoff Evaluation Drug Database (TEDD), enabling patients/doctors to make informed decisions about using provisional drugs versus drugs that have received conventional FDA approval. Anonymized patient characteristics, including genetic data and biomarkers, plus treatment results posted in real time would enable subgroups of patients to be identified that do especially well or poorly. This treasure trove of data is not only useful for patient decisions but also for providing R&D insights for developers of provisional drugs and the biopharmaceutical industry in general.[8] Today's technology is ripe for facilitating freedom of choice.

Drug developers could choose to continue with the conventional FDA track while simultaneously participating on the FTCM track or to continue solely on the FTCM track. That choice partly depends on the developer's financial resources. In addition, the FTCM track focuses on patients who are willing to forego conventional FDA approval and assume higher risk to achieve earlier access. How early they can achieve access depends upon their comfort level with the up-to-date TEDD treatment results.

This is a dynamic self-adjusting system. Expect more patients to use a drug that is generating favorable outcomes and vice versa. Participation is voluntary. Expect a large number of patients to use provisional drugs that have demonstrated superior safety and effectiveness for serious medical conditions. These numbers could easily be in the thousands compared to RCTs that typically have numbers in the hundreds. Big-data analytics/AI applied to TEDD would provide insights in real time. Interestingly, those patients who voluntarily use provisional drugs constitute a heterogeneous universe that is much more likely to identify adverse side effects compared to RCT data with homogeneous patients. Importantly, real-time posting of treatment results and any adverse side effects is uniquely useful for patients/doctors comparing provisional drugs to fully approved drugs. Also, FTCM legislation needs to provide immunity, with the exception for gross negligence, for drug developers and doctors. In addition, insurance companies should be required to treat provisional drugs in the same manner as fully approved drugs.

Importantly, the prices for provisional drugs should be market prices that reflect the drug's safety and effectiveness versus competing drugs. Market prices would incentivize participation by drug developers and help overcome fear by developers that circumventing the conventional clinical testing process could eventually lead to excessive scrutiny by the FDA. Drug developers would be motivated to charge lower prices to gain greater usage and more impressive TEDD data that could bring full FDA approval. Keep in mind that drug developers would be financially able (and competition should compel them) to lower prices since the regulatory costs for provisional drugs would be a small fraction of the costs of conventional approval.

Stepping back from the details of FTCM operation, the system picture is introducing competition to the FDA's status quo. In the private sector, firms and their competitors experiment in an environment of continual fast-paced change. The resulting feedback guides the firm in making changes and adapting. Customers are the ultimate beneficiaries of this process. Since the adoption of RCTs as the FDA's business model, there has been a relentless increase in regulation (and drug prices) without any hard-nosed, objective (feedback) analysis of costs versus benefits that could lead to significant change. The FDA's culture of protecting the status quo and not seeking feedback suggests it is ripe for significant streamlining. After completing his term as FDA commissioner, Andrew von Eschenbach expressed support for commonsense reform like FTCM in a *Wall Street Journal* op-ed (February 14, 2012):

> Breakthrough technologies deserve a breakthrough in the way the FDA evaluates them. Take regenerative medicine. If a company can grow cells that repair the retina in a lab, patients who've been blinded by macular degeneration shouldn't have to wait years while the FDA asks the company to complete laborious clinical trials proving efficacy. Instead, after proof of concept and safety testing, the product should be approved for marketing with every eligible patient entered in a registry [TEDD] so the company and the FDA can establish efficacy through post-market studies.

The takeaway here is that FTCM would provide a useful alternative to the FDA's current regulatory system. This ongoing objective feedback incentivizes change at the FDA to improve efficiency. With FTCM, expect a more streamlined and efficient FDA to evolve over time that is far better suited to an environment of fast-paced medical innovation.

Fast-Paced Innovation Drives Health Improvements and Cures

As previously noted, TEDD provides a treasure trove of real-world data (especially subgroup data) that would lead to both quicker and improved R&D decisions by the biopharmaceutical industry, thereby boosting innovation. This would facilitate funding from venture capitalists who analyze potential investments in both biotech startups and other startups (that don't involve waiting ten years for possible FDA approval). A nascent biotech firm, for example, with leading-edge scientists but little capital might have a revolutionary approach to curing cancer. However, under the status quo, the startup management sees a big opportunity to help patients, while venture capitalists see significant risk in the science, in raising capital in the future, and in navigating clinical trials compounded by a huge delay in achieving a payout (i.e., FDA approval and commercialization). Moreover, a clinical trial may fail to reach the FDA's statistical milestones while revealing subgroups that deliver superb results and potentially provide new insights as to why those subgroups performed as they did. Good luck, says the FDA. Hindsight bias doesn't count, so go raise funds for a new clinical trial.

What happens to a biotech firm with a radically different approach (compared to approved drugs) to developing a potential cure for a serious disease when it enters Phase III clinical testing (see Figure 1)? Two pivotal RCTs need to be successful before the FDA begins its decision-making process. As previously discussed, the FDA will impose especially challenging endpoints for these trials because the firm's approach does not conform to approved drugs, abetted by the FDA's unrelenting fear of negative publicity due to a mistaken approval decision. Of course, for venture capitalists, this renders a potential breakthrough scientific approach even more risky. They are keenly aware of how the startup biotech world is fraught with problems and delays that can decimate a hoped-for, above-average return on their invested capital.

Contrast the previous scenario with FTCM wherein if the science works so that Phase I safety and initial Phase II safety/efficacy are successful, conditional approval could lead to expanded usage, revenues, and real-world data that quickly demonstrates effectiveness for the new drug. For venture capitalists, the FTCM environment is enormously more attractive versus the status quo. This could result in an upsurge of high-risk capital to fund biotech startups thereby scaling up innovation.

Japan's Conditional Approval for Regenerative Medicine Treatments

I received an email in 2007 from Masaru Uchiyama in which he noted his agreement with my rationale for FTCM stated in a pamphlet being circulated by free-market think tanks. He asked for modest funding to translate the pamphlet into Japanese. And he assured me that he personally would deliver this to, and have conversations with, important leaders throughout Japan. I accepted his offer even though I was skeptical about the impact. Three years later, he sent me a short email: "I did what I said I would do."

The FTCM pamphlet translation was instrumental in Japan passing in 2014 a partial version of FTCM (TEDD not initially included). This was a significant step forward for a major country with an exceptionally large population of older people. Japan's conditional approval legislation facilitates early access to innovative new regenerative medicine treatments (e.g., stem cells).

In his article, "Free to Choose Medicine in Japan: A Model for America," Edward Hudgins notes:

> Masaru Uchiyama, president of Japanese for Tax Reform, explained that he heavily promoted a 2007 Japanese translation of an early version of Madden's FTCM book to government ministries and agencies, pharmaceutical companies, medical equipment manufacturers, nongovernment organizations critical to government policy,

pharmacodynamics litigation organizations, etc. He observed local government officials offered support for this approach at parliamentary study meetings.[9]

What explains the ready acceptance of FTCM principles by Japanese leaders? My sense is that their culture embraces doing what is best for elderly patients as a top priority while avoiding an automatic defense of regulatory processes (government knows best).

In their article, "Downgrading of Regulation in Regenerative Medicine," Douglas Sipp and Margaret Sleeboom-Faulkner criticize FTCM in general and Japan's conditional approval in particular, arguing that "sacrificing efficacy requirements for speed is unwise."[10] However, they do not address the tradeoff issue. What is the optimal tradeoff between efficacy testing and faster access with lower prices? No one knows. FTCM provides a mechanism whereby consumer choice allows patients to express what they believe is in their best interests on this tradeoff issue.

Compassionate Use Versus Right to Try

A patient may apply to the FDA for compassionate use (also called expanded access) of a not-yet-approved drug after meeting these criteria:

- Life-threatening condition
- Patient's doctor judges that the risks of the disease outweigh the risks of the not-yet-approved drug
- Inability to enroll in a clinical trial
- Approval by an FDA-approved institutional review board

Keep in mind that in the absence of TEDD-like data, a patient's doctor can only provide a cursory assessment of the risk/opportunity from the new drug. Also, smaller biopharmaceutical firms with limited capital and scarce supply of the new drug might want to avoid being forced to distribute the drug at an FDA-approved price that only recognizes the manufacturing and delivery costs. Agreement with this price may later be used against the developer who wins FDA approval and then sets a price to recoup the huge regulatory costs plus a profit. This can motivate participating developers to not charge for supplying the drug.[11]

Deaths associated with the new drug are worrisome, to say the least, for developers focused on gaining FDA approval. Some developers may conclude that the safer route is to avoid participating in compassionate access and exclusively stick with the FDA's conventional process.

In 2018, President Trump signed the Right to Try bill to improve compassionate access via:

- The patient's doctor's request is sent directly to the drug developer without needing FDA approval or oversight.
- Institutional review board approval is not needed.
- The drug developer can charge a price without needing FDA agreement.

The concerns noted earlier for compassionate use apply equally to Right to Try (i.e., a reluctance to charge for the drug and a perception that the FDA does not welcome circumventing their conventional process). Interestingly, some developers may still prefer compassionate use, feeling the safer route is to get FDA involvement and institutional review board approval.

In conclusion, legislation that implements FTCM principles would improve compassionate access and Right to Try as follows:

- TEDD fills a significant need by enabling patients advised by their doctors to make informed decisions consistent with their health condition and risk preference.
- Insurance firms would be required to treat provisional approval drugs (drugs on the FTCM track, see Figure 7.1) the same as approved drugs (i.e., based on effectiveness and safety in use).
- The FTCM track constitutes a different business model for drug developers in which their regulatory costs are radically reduced and they can charge much lower prices while still achieving profits consistent with the value their drug delivers.

- Drug developers can set prices for the provisional approval drugs consistent with the quantity and quality of TEDD data for treatment results. They would be incentivized to keep prices lower to attract more patients; in addition, as FTCM increases in use as a strategic business model, competition would increase.
- If real-world data in TEDD clearly shows that the provisional approval drug delivers sustained benefits to patients, the FDA may grant full approval—a significant incentive for developers to price provisional drugs at prices (coupled with insurance reimbursement) that are attractive to patients.

FTCM implemented at scale through the voluntary participation of patients advised by their doctors would provide much-needed feedback to assess the FDA's performance in achieving better drugs sooner, and at a lower cost. The FDA is no different from other monopolies that nurture a culture that protects their way of doing things. For the FDA, that means protecting their statistical processes that have been used for decades to facilitate and defend their approval decisions. The earlier op-ed quote from former FDA commissioner Andrew von Eschenbach supports this conclusion. Upon leaving the FDA culture, he speaks his mind (and heart) and recommends FTCM principles. Longer term, competition from FTCM would incentivize the FDA to streamline their regulatory process, thereby boosting FDA efficiency.

One approach to implementing FTCM principles would be to first implement them for a narrow population to gain needed experience. Specifically, patients, doctors, drug developers, and the FDA could gain experience with using TEDD data and the related benefits, including up-to-date treatment results, detailed patient data, and quantification of subgroups who do especially well or poorly using a particular provisional drug. Consistent with this approach, the Promising Pathway Act (PPA) achieved significant bipartisan support in 2024 but was shelved due to the November 2024 election.

The Promising Pathway Act

The PPA is expected to be reintroduced in Congress in 2025. The PPA enables informed choice for patients fighting life-threatening rare and progressive diseases. The PPA provides conditional approval for a maximum of eight years. During this time, if a drug fails to receive full FDA approval via conventional clinical trials, it loses its conditional approval. A database of treatment results (think TEDD) would enable informed decision-making and spotlight the advantages of real-time posting of treatment results for a heterogeneous patient population as opposed to confidential clinical trial data for a homogeneous population. Biopharmaceutical research would benefit from the expedited availability of this data. Similar to FTCM, particularly effective drugs could be granted full approval by the FDA.

Edward Hudgins, founder of the Human Achievement Alliance, and I have worked with Al Musella and Keith Desserich to improve the language of the PPA. Most all of our recommendations were accepted by the bill's sponsors. Musella is a doctor and a computer/database expert. He founded the Musella Foundation for Brain Tumor Research & Information, which maintains a highly regarded database for brain tumor treatment results. At no charge to patients, experts worldwide analyze the patient's data, access the database, and recommend best treatments that invariably include a combination therapy with a not-yet-approved drug. Desserich is a serial entrepreneur who lost his daughter to brain cancer. He and his wife founded The Cure Starts Now, which focuses on research funding for those cancers that offer the biggest opportunities for learning—an innovative strategy that targets cancer cures, not incremental treatment improvements. Keith has been the point person in orchestrating support for the PPA, especially with members of the Senate and the House. His Senate testimony supporting the PPA is contained in a short insightful video: https://www.thecurestartsnow.org/ppa.

Al and Keith have extensive experience in the trenches helping parents with children on death's doorstep. Their experience suggests that the PPA would be far more beneficial than existing options such as compassionate use and Right to Try.

Concluding Thoughts

A friend of mine, Frank Burroughs, lost his daughter Abigail to neck cancer. She was valedictorian of her high school class and died just as her adult life was beginning at age twenty-one. Losing a child is a parent's worst nightmare, but Frank's loss was compounded by the haunting knowledge that Abigail's life might have been saved if only she had access to a breakthrough drug, Erbitux. Abigail's highly regarded oncologist wanted to prescribe Erbitux, but he could not do so legally because Erbitux had not yet been approved by the FDA. Frank tried to get Abigail into a clinical trial for Erbitux, but she did not meet the precise acceptance conditions. Abigail was unable to secure compassionate use from the FDA. Erbitux was eventually approved to treat exactly the type of cancer that Abigail had, but it was too late for her. Such a heart-ripping experience is equal parts tragedy and outrage.

Frank decided to channel his grief and devote his life to helping people battling life-threatening diseases. He cofounded the Abigail Alliance for Better Access to Developmental Drugs to assist patients trying to gain early access to promising therapeutic drugs that are (too) slowly making their way through the FDA's clinical trial process.

A few days before she died, Abigail did an extensive television interview as part of an effort by herself and her father to educate people about the life-and-death consequences of the lack of patient access to promising new drugs. During the interview, Abigail told the audience, "This is not just about me. This is about many others."

The Abigail Alliance sued the FDA to try and establish a constitutional right to save one's life by accessing a not-yet-approved drug. Andrew von Eschenbach was the head of the FDA at that time, and *Abigail Alliance for Better Access to Developmental drugs v. von Eschenbach* reached the Supreme Court. In 2008, the Supreme Court declined to hear the case. Encouragement from Frank and many others has kept me working on the FTCM proposal.

If you are wondering how the economics profession views FTCM, consider Nobel Laureate Vernon Smith's foreword to the third edition of my *Free to Choose Medicine* book:

There is no feedback mechanism to evaluate the benefits versus costs of the hugely expensive and lengthy FDA clinical trials. The negative consequences to society of failing to modify this regulatory process will worsen as the pace of medical innovation accelerates. Hence, the importance of reforms in FDA procedures is overdue.... Madden's market-based solution appeals to economists like me who are keenly aware of the critical importance of [systems thinking] institutional design for a system to promote decentralized responses close to the local knowledge that is available to physicians and their patients, but not to the FDA.... These design components for patient/doctor control of medical treatment are both innovative and soundly based. With Madden's conceptual blueprint, legislation could be crafted to promote both expanded consumer choice and the discipline of choice to the long-term benefit of society.... This book is fundamentally bipartisan and should be read in that spirit.[12]

FTCM can be distilled into the following simple diagram that lays out the synergistic FTCM components to achieve better drugs, sooner, at lower cost.

Figure 7.2: FTCM end results

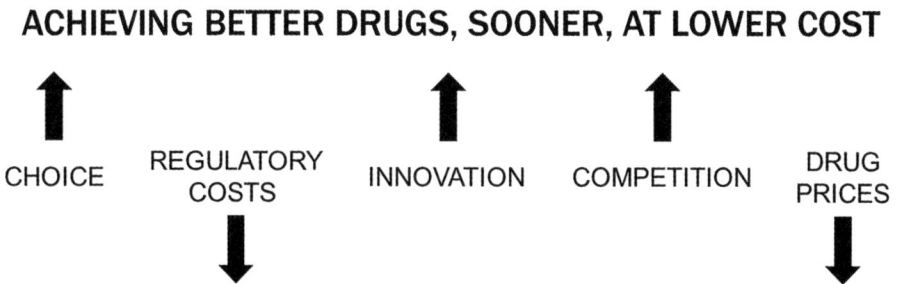

ACHIEVING BETTER DRUGS, SOONER, AT LOWER COST

CHOICE ↑ REGULATORY COSTS ↓ INNOVATION ↑ COMPETITION ↑ DRUG PRICES ↓

There are two ways that FTCM could be a clear win for the FDA while also providing a win-win opportunity for patients and drug developers:

- Early identification of subgroups that do well or poorly using the new drug enables the developer to substantially improve the design of upcoming Phase III trials and dramatically improve the chance for success. This avoids the situation in which, after conventional Phase III testing, the developer has discovered the reasons why certain patients do well and others do poorly but faces the expensive (time and money) prospect of having to do a new trial because the status quo FDA labels this new knowledge as hindsight bias. This way of helping developers improves the efficiency of the FDA's regulatory system.
- Early identification of unusually effective breakthrough drugs for patients in dire need is coupled with TEDD data for a large number of patients. When TEDD data are particularly strong for safety and efficacy of the new drug, the FDA can be confident in immediately granting approval, perhaps with the requirement for continued monitoring of patient treatment results. Big win for the FDA in delivering better drugs sooner at a lower cost.

In conclusion, Free to Choose Medicine resonates with everyone—it's just plain common sense. In the spirit of Vernon Smith's call for bipartisanship, there is support across the political spectrum ready to get behind FDA reform legislation.

CHAPTER 8

Living the Life of a Value Creator

Perhaps the most costly disassembly in which our culture has been engaged is the disaggregation of life itself into work, play, learning, and inspiration. Each of these aspects of life has been separated from the others by creating institutions for engaging in only one at a time, excluding the other three as much as possible. Businesses are designed for work, not play, learning, or inspiration. Country clubs, theatres, and sports stadiums ae designed for play, not work, learning, or inspiration. Schools are designed for learning, not work, play, or inspiration. Museums and churches are designed for inspiration, not work, play, or learning. However, one of the most important products of systems thinking is the realization that the effectiveness with which any of these four functions can be carried out depends on the extent to which they are carried out together, in an integrated way.[1]

—RUSSELL L. ACKOFF

I began a journey as a young man to educate myself about value creation and to communicate what I believed to be useful and not adequately presented in the traditional MBA curriculum. This book offers important takeaways enabling readers to build upon what I have learned.

Four interrelated topics are addressed in this chapter:

- Personal reflections on my educational journey
- New angles on value creation, value capture, and competition
- The Pragmatic Theory of the Firm in the context of the Balanced Scorecard
- Learning to live the life of a value creator

Personal Reflections on My Educational Journey

Occasionally I am asked why I did not continue my formal education and obtain a PhD in finance. Simple answer: I needed to generate income to take care of financial responsibilities. However, that decision led to a hybrid academic career (independent researcher publishing in academic journals) that proved to be significantly more productive than if I had followed a conventional PhD path of publishing to get tenure and then continuing to publish in niche areas of finance as part of a teaching/research career.

My research at Callard, Madden & Associates provided a unique lens to connect a firm's long-term financial performance to its market valuation. For over fifty years, I have intensely studied the life-cycle track records of firms and researched the causal factors. This led me far beyond finance and economics. Not having a teaching load nor a need to publish on specialized finance topics enabled me to sail where the wind blew and to dig deep into systems thinking and knowledge building. My autobiography, *My Value Creation Journey,* describes how I assembled a network of academics in a variety of disciplines who appreciated the journey I was taking and provided valuable feedback on papers that were later published as journal articles. In turn, these articles served as the foundation for a series of monographs and books.[2] In retrospect, these works were stepping stones to eventually assemble the Pragmatic Theory of the Firm.[3] I use the term "theory" because its application can better enable the user to (1) think about value creation by firms; (2) develop insights about a firm's (or a business unit's) historical performance and likely future performance; (3) make managerial decisions that improve future firm performance; and (4) make investment decisions that improve future portfolio performance.

Recall the six key insights noted in the preface and overview:

- Knowledge improvements are a prerequisite to significant value creation.
- Systems thinking complements constructive skepticism about what we think we know.
- The Pragmatic Theory of the Firm views the firm as a holistic system for creating value, which sets the stage for exploring new value creation possibilities. Systems thinking and the pragmatic theory are a hand-in-glove fit.
- Insights about the knowing process via the Knowledge-Building Loop help to better appreciate context, to see problems with alternative perspectives, and to ask better questions.
- Language is perception's silent partner. Attention to language offers an actionable pathway to disentangle the assumptions behind the words.
- Learning to experience alternative ways of seeing (a major benefit of systems thinking) can lead to a changed and improved worldview.

As mentioned in the beginning of this book, I am a visual thinker who strives for pictures to understand and communicate ideas. Hence, the above six insights are illustrated in Figure 8.1.

Figure 8.1: The Knowledge-Building Loop complements the Pragmatic Theory of the Firm

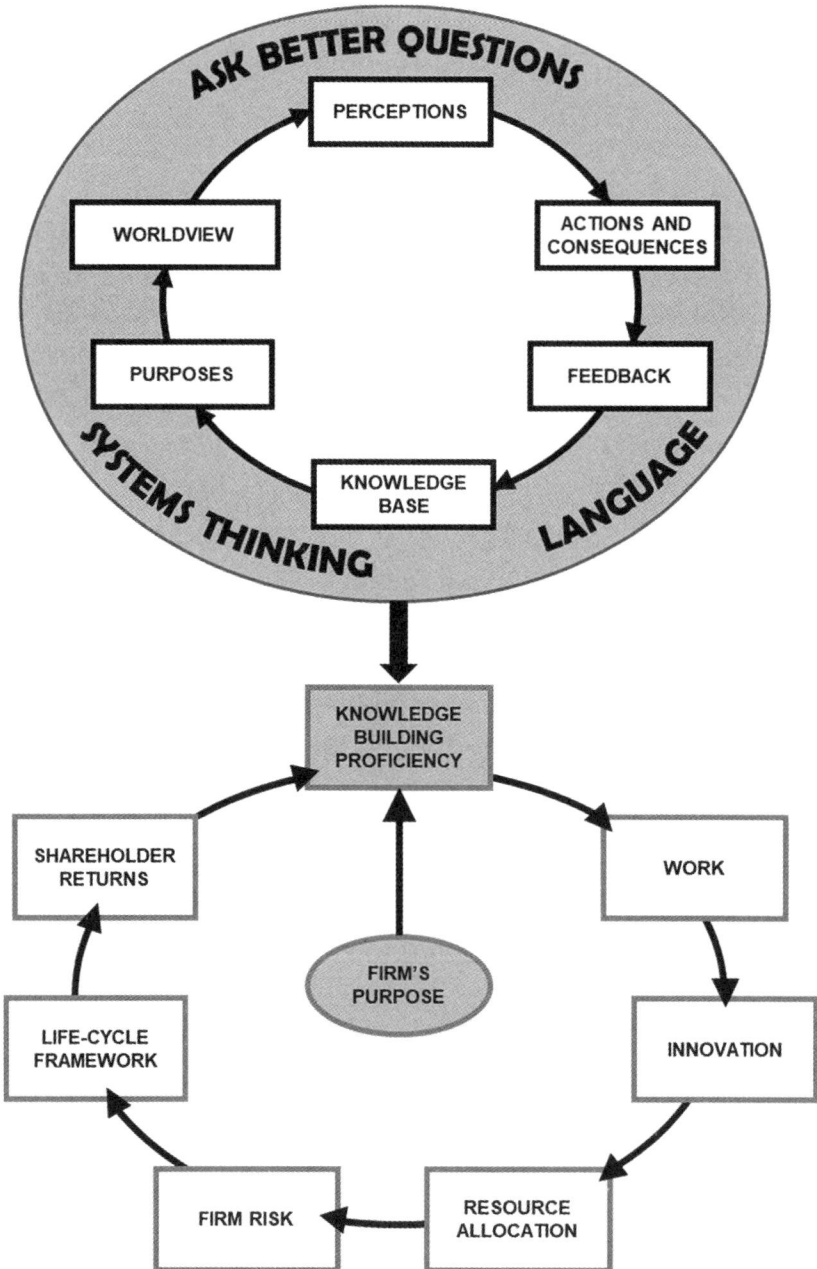

Figure 8.1 condenses my educational journey into a single diagram. Ideally, from my perspective, a reader actively engages with the Knowledge-Building Loop (upper part of Figure 8.1) so that their worldview improves by embracing systems thinking and constructive skepticism about what we think we know.

The knowing steps—which I label knowledge base, purposes, worldview, perceptions, actions and consequences, and feedback—provide guideposts to critique what we think we know. To efficiently get through the day, we necessarily put ourselves on automatic pilot using assumptions from our knowledge base (enabling our brains to conserve energy). Not questioning the assumption, for example, that when cars are perceived as bigger, they are also closer proves very useful. However, as decisions, whether in business or life in general, gain in importance and complexity, constructive skepticism about our knowledge base and the mediating effects of our worldview also gain in importance. Especially for complex problems, we need to examine how our worldview shapes perceptions of problems, solutions, and the data we select for experimentation. Further, we need to systematically seek alternative perspectives for defining problems and for evaluating different ways of achieving the desired outcomes. Systems thinking recognizes complexity (especially for problems involving multiple stakeholders) and sets the table for alternative ways of seeing problems. In addition to explicitly seeking alternative perspectives, we benefit from habitually questioning assumptions hidden by words and asking better questions. The payoff here is big—finding more obsolete assumptions and generating more "Aha!" breakthrough ideas.

The lower part of Figure 8.1 summarizes the Pragmatic Theory of the Firm, which views the firm as a holistic system that places at the center the firm's four-part purpose; identifies knowledge-building proficiency as the critical determinant of a firm's long-term performance; shows the interrelated activities of work, innovation, and resource allocation; and identifies the key elements for dealing with long-term financial performance—firm risk, life-cycle framework, and shareholder returns.

There are two important ways that the upper and lower parts of Figure 8.1 are connected. First, the pragmatic theory spotlights knowledge-building proficiency. Consequently, there is a need for an explicit understanding of the knowing process, which is the Knowledge-Building Loop.

Second, business people (and business school students) would benefit from the adoption of the Pragmatic Theory of the Firm as part of their knowledge base/worldview. Otherwise, people develop an inventory of disconnected assumptions about stock prices and earnings growth rates, maximizing shareholder value, stakeholder interests, competitive advantage, meeting or exceeding Wall Street's quarterly expectations, and, for business school graduates, the mistaken notion that agency theory and adversarial relationships suffice as a viable theory of the firm.

New Perspectives on Value Creation, Value Capture, and Competition

Value creation can be defined subjectively as the experience of purchase/delivery (cost and ease) of a product or service and its usability (efficiently completing what the user wants done) such that the user concludes that this is a good deal. Importantly, firms compete to offer the best value as perceived by customers. However, this restricted view diverts attention away from the complete system, which includes suppliers and collaborators.

In a pioneering article, "Value-Based Business Strategy," Adam Brandenburger and Harborne Stuart note that the user's willingness to pay could be quantified. That is, the buyer is offered the product or service at increasingly higher prices until a price is reached beyond which the buyer feels worse off.[4] Call that point the "willingness to pay." Apply the same process for the supplier to the firm. At declining prices, eventually the supplier concludes that any lower price makes them worse off. Call that point the "opportunity cost" for the supplier. This way of thinking yields total value created as the difference between willingness to pay and opportunity cost and emphasizes the importance of a systems perspective.

Importantly, Brandenburger and Stuart focus on both *value created* and *value captured* while introducing game theory. Their systems perspective is refreshing and important. With this perspective, suppliers compete against other suppliers, and firms compete with one another.

Returning to the total value created, how is this divided? The buyer's (customer's) share is willingness to pay less actual price. The firm's share is actual price less actual cost. Finally, the supplier's share is actual cost to the firm less supplier's opportunity cost. This is diagrammed in Figure 8.2.

Figure 8.2: Value created and value captured

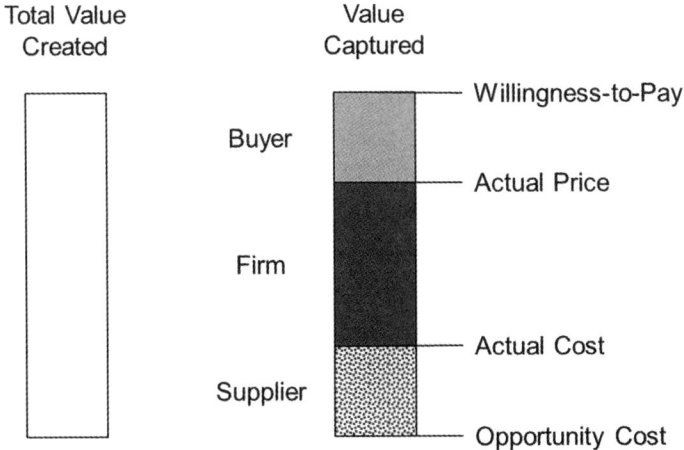

This holistic, strategic way of thinking about the overall system leads to a network view in which suppliers to firms compete against other suppliers, and firms compete with one another. Moreover, on occasion, firms cooperate when it is mutually advantageous.

A key strategic issue is the added value to a network that a firm can contribute. Strategic thinking involves positioning the firm to both better add value and capture value in the context of a network as opposed to a singular focus on product innovation inside the firm (e.g., internal R&D). This entails creativity to help firms more effectively do the jobs customers need done.

The practical importance of this way of thinking was illustrated in 2024 when the farm equipment manufacturer Deere partnered with Elon Musk's SpaceX. Deere provides computer-aided farm equipment to assist farmers in coordinating tasks within short windows of time throughout the year. However, at times farmers face rural loss of connectivity and are unable to leverage Deere's precision agriculture network. SpaceX has built Starlink, a state-of-the-art satellite internet constellation that provides coverage to over one hundred countries. The addition of Starlink to Deere's network creates substantial value for Deere's customers worldwide at little cost to either Deere or SpaceX, so that substantial value is captured by both firms.

In a survey article, "Value Capture Theory: A Strategic Management Review," that extends the pioneering work of Brandenburg and Stuart, Joshua Gans and Michael Ryall highlight several related insights. They describe an emerging science for modeling strategic moves. Their value capture model views competition working in multiple directions and not simply one firm intent on winning more share of a product market while others lose.

Here is a taste of their value capture way of thinking. A value network is a group of agents engaged in transactions (chains) that produce economic value. Firm A's value added to the network is the difference between value produced by the network with the firm versus without—the *upper bound* on A's ability to capture value. If A joins a different network, the increase in that network's value due to including A places a *lower bound* on A's ability to capture value (i.e., the minimum incentive to keep A from joining a different network). In this simple example, the expected value captured by A is between the upper bound and the lower bound.

Gans and Ryall make a compelling case for expanding our thinking beyond some competitors winning while others losing:

> In such a world [finite resources], logic does *not* dictate that the moment some resource becomes a source of value capture for its owner, other agents will reallocate their own resources against it in a tsunami of competition. Rather, economic logic implies that agents allocate *away* from less profitable to more profitable settings, and resource finitude implies that such settings need not be exhausted—*in a finite world, economic profit may well be the rule rather than the exception.* . . . the value capture model suggests that competition is properly construed as placing *bounds* on the amount of value an agent may capture without

> fully determining it. . . . In any given industry, value is created
> and appropriated through complex webs of transactions pursued
> by multiple layers of active, intelligent agents.[5]

In summary, Gans and Ryall's value capture model can explain value creation from a systems perspective. It spotlights the potential advantages from collaborating with other firms (e.g., Deere and SpaceX). It provides insights about the evolution of the Haier Group (discussed in chapter 4) to being the dominant agent (orchestrator) with its platform networked to other firms contributing to the customer experience. This way of thinking has started to change the worldviews of management strategists and their perceptions of opportunities for value creation.

The Pragmatic Theory of the Firm in the Context of the Balanced Scorecard

Here is a relevant question for readers of this book: How can I gain experience with the ideas in this book to determine for myself their degree of usefulness? For those currently working in business, the larger their firm, the more likely that some version of the Balanced Scorecard is being used throughout their organization. This section will show how some of the key ideas covered in the prior chapters can be put to practical use by enhancing the Balanced Scorecard and its focus on successfully implementing a firm's strategy.

In their game-changing article, "The Balanced Scorecard—Measures That Drive Performance," Robert Kaplan and David Norton, in the spirit of the Pragmatic Theory of the Firm, argue:

> Probably because traditional measurement systems have sprung
> from the finance function, the systems have a control bias. That
> is, traditional performance measurement systems specify the
> particular actions they want employees to take and then measure
> to see whether the employees have in fact taken those actions. In

that way, the systems try to control behavior. Such measurement systems fit with the engineering mentality of the Industrial Age.

The balanced scorecard, on the other hand, is well suited to the kind of organization many companies are trying to become. The scorecard puts strategy and vision, not control, at the center. It establishes goals but assumes that people will adopt whatever behaviors and take whatever actions are necessary to arrive at those goals. The measures are designed to pull people toward the overall vision. Senior managers may know what the end result should be, but they cannot tell employees exactly how to achieve that result, if only because the conditions in which employees operate are constantly changing.[6]

In addition, Kaplan and Norton cogently argue for managers to appreciate interrelationships and avoid the optimization of a part if this will prove detrimental to the whole. The four key perspectives of the Balanced Scorecard are customer, internal processes, learning and growth, and financial. Kaplan and Norton emphasize that traditional financial measures used to control the firm are backward-looking. The Balanced Scorecard is forward-looking and quantifies answers to the following questions:

- What is the customer value proposition?
- What internal processes must we excel at?
- To achieve our vision, how do we sustain needed learning and growth?
- How do shareholders benefit from successful strategy execution?

Kaplan and Norton's work was extended by linking strategy formulation and implementation. The Balanced Scorecard was paired with the Strategy Map, which shows cause-and-effect relationships for the four objectives.[7] This pairing completed the goal of enabling a performance measurement system to become a strategy-based management system as diagrammed in Figure 8.3.

Figure 8.3: The Strategy Map is a needed complement to the Balanced Scorecard

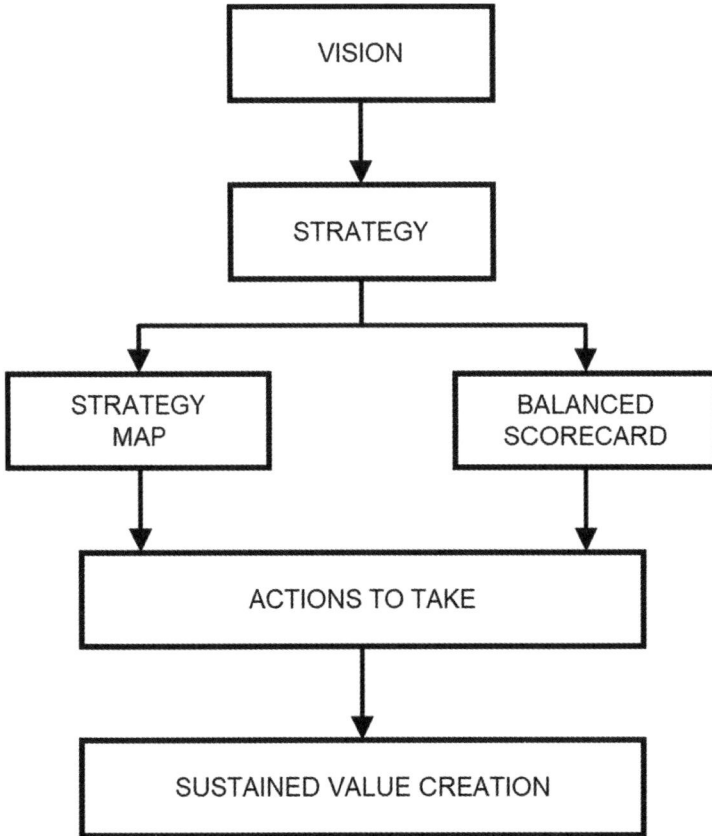

```
                    ┌──────────────────────┐
                    │        VISION         │
                    └──────────────────────┘
                               │
                               ▼
                    ┌──────────────────────┐
                    │       STRATEGY        │
                    └──────────────────────┘
                       │              │
              ┌────────┘              └────────┐
              ▼                                ▼
   ┌──────────────────┐           ┌──────────────────┐
   │    STRATEGY       │           │    BALANCED       │
   │      MAP          │           │   SCORECARD       │
   └──────────────────┘           └──────────────────┘
              │                                │
              ▼                                ▼
   ┌──────────────────────────────────────────────────┐
   │                ACTIONS TO TAKE                     │
   └──────────────────────────────────────────────────┘
                               │
                               ▼
   ┌──────────────────────────────────────────────────┐
   │            SUSTAINED VALUE CREATION                │
   └──────────────────────────────────────────────────┘
```

There are three proposed enhancements to the Balanced Scorecard/ Strategy Map shown in Figure 8.3. Beginning at the top, expand vision to gain absolute clarity as to the purpose of the firm, as discussed in chapter 1.[8] The four-part purpose used in the Pragmatic Theory of the Firm resolves the endless debates about shareholder capitalism versus stakeholder capitalism, provides guideposts for environmental, social, and governance initiatives, and includes a vision that can motivate employees to enthusiastically commit their careers to making the firm successful.

Second, the analysis of organizational structure in chapter 4 suggests that whatever the strategy, successful implementation is easier to achieve with a culture of knowledge-building proficiency (fast learning). Kaplan and Norton agree and include learning and growth as a key perspective for the Balanced Scorecard. However, our analysis suggests that organizational structure is an integral part of both strategy formulation and implementation. This is evident from the examples used in chapter 4.

Nucor's relatively flat structure provides autonomy and resources for their business units to adapt to change. This led to entering the market for high-strength automotive steel. This strategy began with bottom-up adaptation to a changing environment and was facilitated by top management quickly providing capital for a large-scale plant expansion. At a deeper level, this strategy was the result of Nucor's organizational structure.

Haier Group's ultraflat organizational structure led to Haier's networked platform that coordinates thousands of microenterprises plus outside collaborators to seize opportunities for value creation. Structure and strategy are intertwined. The platform enables Haier to capture a sizable part of the value created by its platform while sustaining a unique competitive advantage.

Bayer's current core strategy is to radically restructure its bureaucratic command-and-control structure while dealing with significant problems due to a strategic blunder in acquiring Monsanto. One lesson from Bayer is that it is likely that most large firms operate with excessive layers of management control. Consequently, strategy and structure need to be addressed simultaneously. Easier said than done. Top management surely is uncomfortable with the prospect of restructuring that sharply reduces their control. Keep in mind that they earned their top management positions by excelling in the command-and-control environment. This is also true for most members of the board of directors. Consequently, while significant change in organizational structure has the potential for much improved performance, it probably is the single toughest challenge for both top management and the board to execute.

Figure 8.4 illustrates the proposed enhancements to the Balanced Scorecard—expand vision, treat organizational structure and strategy as intertwined, and incorporate life-cycle track records for the overall firm and especially for its individual business units.

Figure 8.4: Purpose, organizational structure, and life-cycle track records

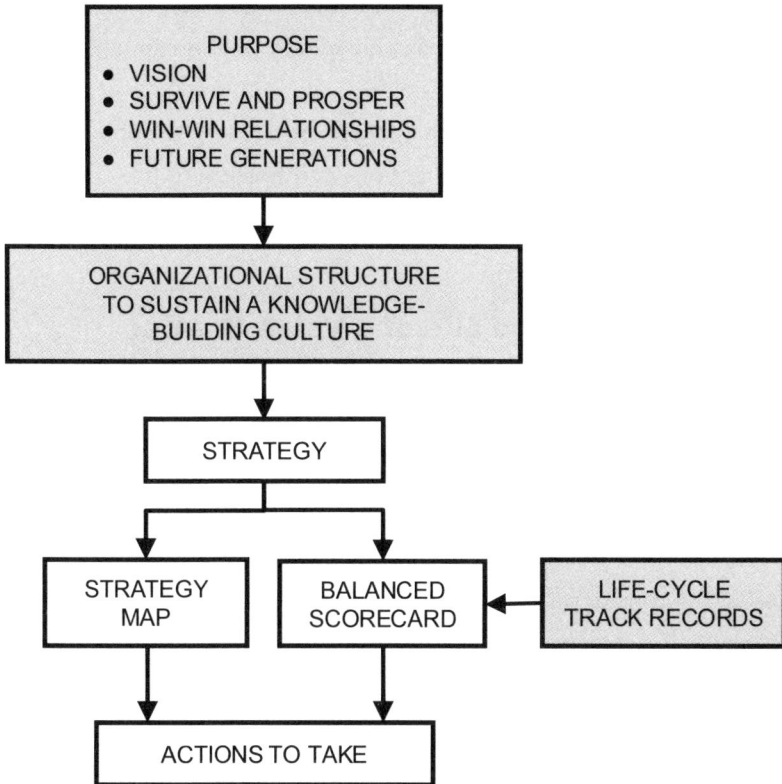

Why choose life-cycle track records over economic value-added (EVA) track records? EVA gains simplicity by compressing all the life-cycle variables into a single number but with a cost,[9] specifically:

- Typically, EVA is computed using some version of the CAPM/ beta cost of capital. But these cost-of-capital estimates are subject to wide variation and can easily cause a switch from a positive to negative EVA, which is often not appreciated by managers who use EVA data.
- When studying EVA track records, users are unaware if an observed increase in EVA is due to a higher reinvestment rate in above-cost-of-capital projects or a reduction in below-cost-of-capital projects. Simplicity comes at a cost.

The above problems are avoided with life-cycle track records that provide a clear visual explanation of the interrelated effects on value creation of economic returns (returns on capital), cost of capital, and reinvestment rates.

The next section discusses the benefit from using the above recommendations to begin gaining experience and to learn to live the life of a value creator.

Learning to Live the Life of a Value Creator

My educational journey has been about seeking a deeper understanding of firm performance and long-term value creation. I learned that knowledge building and value creation are opposite sides of the same coin. What motivates employees to build knowledge that contributes to their team's success? Is there one word that hits the nail on the head? My choice is *freedom*—a word typically associated with social causes and not a firm's organizational structure.

Our analysis of Nucor's flat organizational structure noted the importance of freedom for Ken Iverson, Nucor's chief architect and thirty-year CEO. Iverson focused on shaping an environment that frees employees to determine what they can do and what they should do to benefit themselves and Nucor. Gary Hamel and Michele Zanini's assessment of Nucor also spotlights freedom (i.e., the opportunity to *be a value creator*):

> Nucor's [organizational structure] has been built to maximize creativity, competence, collaboration, commitment, and courage. Not coincidentally, it is these human attributes and behaviors that are most critical to producing extraordinary results. . . . Nucor's [structure] isn't about pushing employees to *do* more, but giving them the opportunity to *be* more—more than blue-collar workers, more than order takers, more than mere operators, more than employees. Nucor's frontline team members are experts, innovators, risk takers, and owners. Nucor proves unequivocally that *every* job can be a good job, whatever the industry.[10]

In summary, a firm's organizational structure should be designed to facilitate a network of rules (including informal rules based on culture and social norms) and conversations that further the achievement of the firm's purpose. This network constitutes a firm's knowledge-building culture. The ideal end result is people who are free to live the life of a value creator, of which they are the architect, to the mutual benefit of themselves and the firm's stakeholders. Is this the substance of what students learn in business school? Not really. In his influential article, "Bad Management Theories Are Destroying Good Management Practices," Sumantra Ghoshal explains the source of management theories taught in business schools:

> If the value creation is achieved by combining the resources of both employees and shareholders, why should the value distribution favor only the latter? Why must the mainstream of our theory be premised on maximizing the returns to just one of these contributors? . . . The answer—the only answer that is really valid—is that this assumption helps in structuring and solving nice mathematical models. Casting shareholders in the role of "principals" who are the equivalent to owners or proprietors, and managers as "agents" who are self-centered and are only interested in using company resources to their own advantage is justified simply because, with this assumption, the elegant mathematics of principal-agent models can be applied to the enormously complex economic, social, and moral issues related to the governance of giant public corporations that have such enormous influence on the lives of . . . millions of people.[11]

We need a more viable theory of the firm than agency theory. This book provides one. It will prove useful by helping readers on their journey to live the life of a value creator. Consider a course on leadership in which students learn about what successful leaders do and how unsuccessful leaders fall short. In contrast, Werner Erhard, Michael Jensen, and collaborators designed and taught a leadership course with the objective that participants leave being leaders.[12] This is about the difference between a student in the classroom learning about the principles (physics) of hitting tennis balls versus being a competent tennis player on the court.

I offer two ways to help readers expedite their journey in being a value creator.

First, those currently in business who read/study this book are probably intellectually curious about new perspectives that might improve their work skills. Their task is to adopt the Pragmatic Theory of the Firm and the related Knowledge-Building Loop to experience benefits in defining and solving problems and improving some of the processes used in their firm. The prior section on the Balanced Scorecard suggested that performance measurement of business units would be upgraded by including life-cycle track records. In turn, this necessitates changes to internal accounting systems to improve the measurement of intangibles (chapter 6). This can be a big win for better resource allocations and analyses of strategic acquisition candidates, plus an intuitive way to visually understand what drives market valuations. Moreover, adoption of the Pragmatic Theory of the Firm both clarifies the firm's four-part purpose and the need to evolve the firm's organizational structure to best implement strategy as laid out in the Balanced Scorecard framework (Figure 8.4).

Second, business school students who read/study this book could better integrate their currently siloed classes, including finance, accounting, economics, strategy, marketing, production processes, leadership/ethics/ corporate governance, and business history. Reaching business school students at scale would likely require the dean and faculty of business schools to conclude that a viable theory of the firm needs to be taught at the beginning of a student's educational journey. Teaching the Pragmatic Theory of the Firm alongside competing theories of the firm would likely be the optimal method of assuring that students learn to live the life of a value creator.

Appendix

Commencement Address

Florida Atlantic University Business School

December 16, 2021

Bartley J. Madden

I am honored to be asked to speak at your graduation ceremony, to share my thoughts, and be with all of you on this special day. As I have walked around the campus of this growing university, I feel the energy, the spirit, the sense of hope, and the excitement about the future.

I began my career as an engineer and then served in the army during the Vietnam War. I concluded that a career in business was right for me, and I then earned my MBA. That graduate degree opened a world of exciting possibilities for me. Your hard work in earning your graduate degree will lead to similar exciting opportunities for you to make the world a better place.

Most of my career has focused on researching the performance of business firms, the connection between long-term firm performance and market valuation, and the over-riding imperative of a knowledge-building, value creation culture.

What I have come to believe is that value creation is the foundation for a prosperous society. With value creation as a guidepost, we are better equipped to transcend the polarization epitomized by capitalism versus socialism or Republican versus Democrat. We can build a more civil society where we seek to build knowledge, to create value for others, and to ensure that no one is left behind. And, for sure, I am excited about the work that will be done by the new value creation center in the college of business at Florida Atlantic University.

I encourage you to commit your working careers to being value creators who continually build knowledge and strive for win-win relationships always. Value creation is about efficiently doing work that contributes to what a customer or client wants or what a patient needs. Nonvalue-adding work is waste. A value creation culture is rooted in constructive skepticism about what we think we know to be true and a desire to experiment and discover root causes of problems.

I have four recommendations as to planning your long-term working careers. First, here is the key question: Will working for this organization better improve my problem-solving skills and expand my knowledge base versus alternative opportunities?

Second, be wary of working for highly bureaucratic organizations with a pyramid command-and-control organizational structure and excessive management layers. In these organizations, typically the next level down does whatever it takes to meet the accounting-based performance goals of the next level up. In this type of environment, lower-level employees are not mentored to improve their problem-solving skills. The result: work easily becomes a real grind.

Third, seek employment in organizations where the culture supports you and where you will be mentored and have opportunities to improve your skills. Avoid organizations where people at the top think they have all the answers. Be adventurous in which industries you consider while looking for organizations where your work could genuinely create value for customers, clients, and patients.

When you have an opportunity to talk with employees of a particular organization, ask probing questions that can reveal if the culture is one of doing whatever it takes to make the numbers and looking for your manager to devise a workaround for significant problems that you encounter. Or, is the culture one of mentoring employees to develop their problem-solving skills so that employees continually expand their knowledge base? The preferred culture will tend to be encountered in flatter organizations versus pyramid command-and-control organizations.

Fourth, you want to work at organizations that will prosper in the future and offer more opportunities for advancement. Spend time reading what the CEO says about the purpose of their organizations. For publicly traded firms, read the shareholder letters written by the CEOs, which are in the firm's annual report, and any other material you can find. This will also help for job interviews. You are looking for a knowledge-building, value creation culture that avoids business-as-usual complacency and instead questions core assumptions, takes pride in experimentation, and adapts early to a changing world.

On my list of the best CEOs of all time are Ken Iverson of Nucor (a steel company noted for its flat organizational structure) and Brad Smith of Intuit (consumer financial software and developer of QuickBooks). Iverson noted: "We anticipate and accept that roughly half of our investments in new ideas and new technologies will yield no usable results. . . . Our managers focus on shaping an environment that frees employees to determine what they can do and should do to the benefit of themselves and the business." Smith noted: "Our rapid experimentation culture cuts through hierarchy . . . creating an environment where everyone can innovate, and debate turns into doing."

These quotes are emblematic of the type of culture in which employees have the freedom to create value to the benefit of all of the organization's stakeholders.

In conclusion, let today's graduation mark the beginning of a journey to live the life of a value creator—all the while striving for win-win relationships. And, in so doing, you certainly can make the world a better place.

Endnotes

Chapter 1

1   Colin Mayer, *Capitalism and Crises: How to Fix Them* (Oxford: Oxford University Press, 2024), 26.

2   For a comprehensive discussion of stock and flow diagrams, see John D. Sterman, *Business Dynamics: Systems Thinking and Modeling for a Complex World* (New York: Irwin McGraw-Hill, 2000).

3   Michael C. Jackson, *Critical Systems Thinking and the Management of Complexity* (Hoboken, NJ: John Wiley & Sons, 2019), xix.

4   Russell L. Ackoff, *Re-Creating the Corporation* (Oxford: Oxford University Press, 1999).

5   Donella H. Meadows, *Thinking in Systems* (White River Junction, Vermont: Chelsea Green Publishing Company, 2008).

6   Jay W. Forrester, *Urban Dynamics* (Cambridge, MA: MIT Press, 1969).

7   Michael C. Jackson, *Critical Systems Thinking: A Practitioner's Guide* (Hoboken, NJ: John Wiley & Sons, 2024).

8   John Seddon, *Freedom from Command and Control: A Better Way to Make the Work Work* (Buckingham, UK: Vanguard Education, Ltd., 2003), 50–51.

9   John Micklethwait and Adrian Wooldridge, *The Company: A Short History of a Revolutionary Idea* (New York: Modern Library, 2003), xv.

10 Ronald Coase, "The Nature of the Firm," *Economica* 4, no. 16 (1937): 386–405.

11 Quote from Thomas W. Hazlett, "Looking for Results: An Interview with Ronald Coase," *Reason*, January 1997.

12 Oliver E. Williamson, "The Economics of Organizations: The Transaction Cost Approach," *American Journal of Sociology* 87, no. 3 (1981): 548–577.

13 Sanford Grossman and Oliver Hart, "The Costs and Benefits of Ownership: A Theory of Vertical and Lateral Integration," *Journal of Political Economy* 94, no. 4 (1986): 691–719.

14 Jay Barney, "Firm Resources and Sustained Competitive Advantage," *Journal of Management* 17, no. 1 (1991): 99–120.

15 Jay. B. Barney, "Where Does Inequality Come From? The Personal and Intellectual Roots of Resource-Based Theory," in *Great Minds in Management: The Process of Theory Development*, eds. Ken G. Smith and Michael A. Hitt (Oxford: Oxford University Press, 2005), 295.

16 Robert M. Grant, "Toward a Knowledge-Based Theory of the Firm," *Strategic Management Journal* 17 (1996, special winter issue): 109–122. Grant agrees with the emphasis on individuals as the foundational unit of analysis for knowledge building (see chapter 2).

17 Robert M. Grant, "Knowledge and Organization," in *Managing Industrial Knowledge: Creation, Transfer, and Utilization*, eds. Ikujiro Nonaka and David Teece (London: Sage Publications, 2001), 165.

18 David J. Teece, "Knowledge Assets, Capabilities, and the Theory of the Firm," chapter 23, in *Handbook of Organizational Learning and Knowledge Management*, eds. Mark Easterly-Smith and Marjorie A. Lyles (Hoboken, NJ: John Wiley & Sons, 2011).

19 Michael C. Jensen and William H. Meckling, "Theory of the Firm: Managerial Behavior, Agency Costs and Ownership Structure," *Journal of Financial Economics* 3, no. 4 (1976): 305–360.

20 R. Edward Freeman, *Strategic Management: A Stakeholder Approach* (New York: HarperCollins, 1984).

21 Michael C. Jensen, *A Theory of the Firm: Governance, Residual Claims, and Organizational Forms* (Cambridge, MA: Harvard University Press, 2000).

22 For a comprehensive reply to critics, see Micael C. Jensen and Kevin J. Murphy, "CEO Incentives: It's Not How Much You Pay, But How," *Harvard Business Review* (1990, May-June): 138–153.

23 Michael C. Jensen and Clifford W. Smith Jr., "Stockholder, Manager, and Creditor Interests: Applications of Agency Theory," in *Recent Advances in Corporate Finance,* eds. E. I. Altman and M. G. Subrahmanyam (Homewood, IL: Irwin, 1985).

24 Michael C. Jensen, "Organization Theory and Methodology," *Accounting Review* 58, no. 2 (1983): 319–339.

25 Michael C. Jensen, "Foreword," in *Moral Markets: The Critical Role of Values in the Economy,* ed. Paul J. Zak (Princeton, NJ: Princeton University Press, 2008), ix–x.

26 See Bartley J. Madden and Douglas E. Stevens, "Michael Jensen's Contributions to the Theory of the Firm: A Tribute in Three Acts," *Journal of Applied Corporate Finance* 36, no. 3 (2024): 117–125.

27 Bartley J. Madden, *Value Creation Principles: The Pragmatic Theory of the Firm Begins with Purpose and Ends with Sustainable Capitalism* (Hoboken, NJ: John Wiley & Sons, 2020), 26–27.

28 James P. Womack and Daniel T. Jones, *Lean Thinking: Banish Waste and Create Wealth in Your Corporation,* 2nd ed. (New York: Free Press, 2003).

29 Mike Rother, *Toyota Kata: Managing People for Improvement, Adaptiveness, and Superior Results* (New York: McGraw Hill, 2010), 165.

30 Jeanne Liedtka, Andrew King, and Kevin Bennett, *Solving Problems with Design Thinking: 10 Stories of What Works* (New York: Columbia University Press, 2013), 183–184.

31 Bartley J. Madden, 2020, p. 107. Also see chapter 8 of David R. Koenig, *The Board Member's Guide to Risk* (Northfield, Minnesota: Bright Governance Publications, 2020).

32 Bartley J. Madden, *My Value Creation Journey: An Autobiography of My Work* (Naples, FL: Bartley J. Madden Foundation, 2024).

33 Key individuals left Callard, Madden & Associates and formed HOLT Value Associates in 1985, which was later acquired by Credit Suisse in 2002. UBS acquired Credit Suisse in 2023.

34 *Bloomberg Businessweek,* "Bezos on Innovation," interview, April 16, 2008.

35 The real cost of capital was estimated at 5.95 percent in Eugene F. Fama and Kenneth R. French, "The Corporate Cost of Capital and the Return on Corporate Investment," *Journal of Finance* 54, no. 6 (1999): 1939–1967.

36 CFROI® is a registered trademark of HOLT, a subsidiary of UBS. Bartley J. Madden, *CFROI Valuation: A Total System to Valuing the Firm*, chapter 5 (Oxford, UK: Butterworth-Heinemann, 1999); David A. Holland and Bryant A. Matthews, *Beyond Earnings: Applying the HOLT CFROI and Economic Profit Framework*, chapter 3 (Hoboken, NJ: John Wiley & Sons, 2018).

37 Elizabeth Brayer, *George Eastman: A Biography* (Rochester, NY: University of Rochester Press, 2006).

38 Edgar H. Schein, *Organizational Culture and Leadership*, 4th ed. (San Francisco, CA: Jossey-Bass, 2010), 18.

39 Douglas E. Stevens, *Social Norms and the Theory of the Firm: A Foundational Approach* (Cambridge, UK: Cambridge University Press, 2019).

40 Milton Friedman, *Essays in Positive Economics* (Chicago: University of Chicago Press, 1953), 8–9.

41 For a critique of Friedman's methodology, see Bartley J. Madden, "A Transactional Approach to Economic Research," *Journal of Socio-Economics* 20, no. 1 (1991): 57–71. For personal correspondence between Friedman and the author regarding this critique, see https://www.learningwhatworks.com/papers/MiltonFriedman%20_2_.pdf.

42 Bartley J. Madden and Douglas E. Stevens, "Extending the Pragmatic Theory of the Firm with Social Norms," *Journal of Applied Corporate Finance*, forthcoming 2025.

43 Claus Dierksmeier, "Reorienting Management Education: From the Homo Economicus to Human Dignity," in *Business Schools Under Fire, Humanistic Management Education as the Way Forward*, eds. W. Amann, M. Pirson, C. Dierksmeier, E. von Kimakowitz, H. Spitzeck, eds. (Houndmills: Palgrave Macmillan, 2011), 19–40.

44 Brad Smith, "The Most Important Job of a CEO," Investors.intuit.com, accessed March 13, 2016.

45   Roger L. Martin, "The Innovation Catalysts," *Harvard Business Review*, June 2011.

Chapter 2

1   Beau Lotto, *Deviate: The Science of Seeing Differently* (New York: Hachette Books, 2017), 118–119.

2   See Bartley J. Madden, *Value Creation Principles: The Pragmatic Theory of the Firm Begins with Purpose and Ends with Sustainable Capitalism*, chapter 3 (Hoboken, NJ: John Wiley & Sons, 2020), for application of the Loop to analyze and contrast three approaches to improving firm performance: lean thinking, Goldratt's theory of constraints, and the Erhard-Jensen ontological/phenomenological model.

3   Ray Dalio, *Principles* (New York: Simon & Schuster, 2017), 188.

4   Dewey and Ames are discussed in Bartley J. Madden, "A Transactional Approach to Economic Research," *Journal of Socio-Economics* 20, no. 1 (1991): 57–71.

5   John Dewey, *Experience and Nature: The Kappa Delta Pi Lecture* (New York: Collier-Macmillan, 1969), 69.

6   Bartley J. Madden, "Management's Worldview: Four Critical Points about Reality, Language, and Knowledge Building to Improve Organization Performance," *Journal of Organizational Computing and Electronic Commerce* 22, no. 4 (2012): 334–346.

7   Donella H. Meadows, *Thinking in Systems* (White River Junction, VT: Chelsa Green Publishing Company, 2008), 164.

8   John Dewey, *Experience and Nature* (New York: Dover Publications, 1958). Dewey's emphasis on continuity and avoiding the separation of perceivers from their perceptions failed to stem psychology's subsequent embrace of a stimulus (perception)/response (action) approach to human behavior. A different perspective (perceptual control theory) is summarized in Bartley J. Madden, *A Foundational Explanation of Human Behavior* (Naples, FL: Bartley J. Madden Foundation, 2021). The basic idea is that your brain controls input perceptions through actions to reduce the discrepancy between what you are perceiving

and what you want to experience. For related insights, see Andreas K. Engel, Karl J. Friston, and Dancia Kragic, *The Pragmatic Turn: Toward Action-Oriented Views in Cognitive Science* (Cambridge, MA: MIT Press, 2015).

9   Andy Clark, *The Experience Machine: How Our Minds Predict and Shape Reality* (New York: Pantheon Books, 2023), 212–213.

10 Matthew Syed, *Black Box Thinking: Why Most People Never Learn from Their Mistakes—but Some Do* (New York: Portfolio/Penguin, 2015), 283.

11 Beau Lotto, *Deviate: The Science of Seeing Differently* (New York: Hachette Books, 2017), 68–69.

12 Lera Boroditsky, "Operational Perceptual Freedom," in *What Have You Changed Your Mind About?* ed. John Brockman (New York: Harper Perennial, 2009), 342–343.

13 John D. Sterman, *Business Dynamics: Systems Thinking and Modeling for a Complex World* (New York: Irwin McGraw-Hill, 2000), 28–29.

14 Stephen M. Shapiro, *Invisible Solutions* (Herndon, VA: Amplify Publishing, 2020), 26.

15 Richard P. Rumelt, *Good Strategy Bad Strategy: The Difference and Why It Matters* (New York: Crown Business, 2011), 23–28.

16 William Duggan, *Creative Strategy: A Guide for Innovation* (NY: Columbia University Press, 2013), 2.

17 Martin Reeves and Jack Fuller, *The Imagination Machine: How to Spark New Ideas and Create Your Company's Future* (Boston, MA: Harvard Business Review Press, 2021).

18 L. David Marquet, *Turn the Ship Around! A True Story of Turning Followers into Leaders* (New York: Penguin Group, 2015), 84.

19 David G. McCullough, *The Wright Brothers* (New York: Simon & Schuster, 2015), 27.

20 Wilbur Wright and Orville Wright, *Miracle at Kitty Hawk*, ed. Fred C. Kelly (New York: Da Capo Press, 1996), 189.

21 Wilbur Wright and Orville Wright, *The Papers of Wilbur and Orville Wright: Including the Chanute-Wright Papers*, 2 vols, ed. Marvin W. McFarland (New York: McGraw-Hill, 2001).

22 David G. McCullough, *The Wright Brothers* (New York: Simon & Schuster, 2015), 65.

23 Peter L. Jakab, *Visions of a Flying Machine: The Wright Brothers and the Process of Invention* (Washington, DC: Smithsonian Institution Press, 1990), 156.

24 Peter L. Jakab, *Visions of a Flying Machine: The Wright Brothers and the Process of Invention* (Washington, DC: Smithsonian Institution Press, 1990), 213.

Chapter 3

1 Rita McGrath, *Seeing Around Corners: How to Spot Inflection Points in Business* (Boston: Houghton Mifflin Harcourt, 2019), 51–52, 56.

2 Martin Reeves and Jack Fuller, *The Imagination Machine: How to Spark New Ideas and Create Your Company's Future* (Boston, MA: Harvard Business Review Press, 2021).

3 Joseph A. Schumpeter, *Capitalism, Socialism, and Democracy* (New York: Harper & Brothers, 1942).

4 Amar Bhide, *Uncertainty and Enterprise: Venturing Beyond the Known* (New York: Oxford University Press, 2025), 36–37.

5 Amy Edmondson, "Learning from Mistakes Is Easier Said Than Done: Group and Organization Influences on the Detection and Correction of Human Error," *Journal of Applied Behavioral Science* 32, no. 1 (1996): 5–28.

6 Matthew Syed, *Black Box Thinking: Why Most People Never Learn from Their Mistakes—but Some Do* (New York: Portfolio/Penguin, 2015).

7 For an especially comprehensive analysis of systems thinking and logic trees, see H. William Dettmer, *The Logical Thinking Process: A Systems Approach to Complex Problem Solving* (Milwaukee, WI: ASQ Quality Press, 2007).

8 Charles Conn and Robert McLean, *Bulletproof Problem Solving: The One Skill That Changes Everything* (Hoboken, NJ: John Wiley & Sons, 2018), 104.

9   Michael Balle, Nicolas Chartier, Pascale Coignet, Sandrine Olivencia, Daryl Powell, and Elvind Reke, *The Lean Sensei: Go See Challenge* (Boston, MA: Lean Enterprise Institute, 2019), 10.

10 Frederick Herzberg, "One More Time: How Do You Motivate Employees?," *Harvard Business Review* 46, no. 1 (January 1968): 52–62.

11 Mike Rother and John Shook, *Learning to See: Value-Stream Mapping to Create Value and Eliminate Muda* (Cambridge, MA: Lean Enterprise Institute, 2003).

12 Curtis R. Carlson and William W. Wilmont, *Innovation: The Five Disciplines for Creating What Customers Want* (New York: Crown Business, 2006).

13 Curtis R. Carlson, "Innovation for Impact," *Harvard Business Review*, November–December 2020.

14 Carlson, 2020.

15 Steve Blank, "Why the Lean Start-Up Changes Everything," *Harvard Business Review*, May 2013.

16 For example, Alexander Osterwalder and Yves Pigneur, *Business Model Generation* (Hoboken, NJ: John Wiley & Sons, 2010); Marc Gruber and Sharon Tal, *Where to Play* (Upper Saddle River, NJ: FT Publishing International, 2017).

17 Steve Blank and Jonathan T. Eckhardt, "The Lean Startup as an Actionable Theory of Entrepreneurship," *Journal of Management* (2024).

18 Teppo Felin, Alfonso Gambardella, Scott Stern, and Todd Zenger, "Lean Startup and the Business Model: Experimentation Revisited," *Long Range Planning* (2020).

19 Teppo Felin, Jan Koenderink, and Joachim I. Krueger, "Rationality, Perception, and the All-Seeing Eye," *Psychonomic Bulletin and Review* (2017). For dissenting views and replies, see Nick Chater et al., "Mind, Rationality, and Cognition: An Interdisciplinary Debate," *Psychonomic Bulletin and Review* (2017).

20 Teppo Felin, Alfonso Gambardella, Elena Novelli, and Todd Zenger, "A Scientific Method for Startups," *Journal of Management* (2024).

21 Mark Packard, *Entrepreneurial Valuation: An Entrepreneurial Guide to Getting into the Minds of Customers* (Berlin: De Gruyter, 2022), 129.

22 Tojin T. Eapen, Daniel J. Finkenstadt, Josh Folk, and Lokesh Venkataswamy, "How Generative AI Can Augment Human Creativity," *Harvard Business Review* 101, no. 4 (2023): 56–75.

23 Tony McCaffrey and Jim Pearson, "Find Innovation Where You Least Expect It," *Harvard Business Review* (December 2015): 82–89.

24 See chapter 6 in Tony McCaffrey, *Overcome Any Obstacle to Creativity* (Lanham, Maryland: Rowman & Littlefield, 2018).

Chapter 4

1 Rita McGrath and Ram Charan, "The Permissionless Corporation," *Harvard Business Review* (January–February 2023).

2 For an up-to-date global source of information about self-managing (flat) organizations, see https://www.corporaterebels.com.

3 Bartley J. Madden, "Management's Key Responsibility," *Journal of Applied Corporate Finance* 30, no. 3 (2018): 27–35.

4 Brian Maskell and Nicholas Katko, "Value Stream Costing: The Lean Solution to Standard Costing Complexity and Waste," in *Lean Accounting: Best Practices for Sustainable Integration*, ed. Joe Stenzel (Hoboken, NJ: John Wiley & Sons, 2007), 155–157. Their book offers useful discussions for transitioning to a lean cost accounting system.

5 Daniel Benjamin and David Komlos, "CEO of Roche Pharmaceuticals on Serving Patients during the Pandemic and Driving Transformational Change," *Forbes*, interview, July 29, 2020. Also see a video interview with Gary Hamel and Michele Zanini, https://www.garyhamel.com/video/busting-bureaucracy-bill-anderson.

6 Bjarte Bogsnes, *This Is Beyond Budgeting: A Guide to More Adaptive and Human Organizations* (Hoboken, NJ: John Wiley & Sons, 2023). See Beyond Budgeting's website: www.bbrt.org.

7 Joost Minnaar, Pim de Porree, and Bram der Lecq, *Start-Up Factory: Haier's RenDanHeyi Model and the End of Management as We Know It* (Eindhoven, NL: Corporate Rebels, 2022).

8   For additional insights, see Venkat Atluri and Miklos Dietz, *The Ecosystem Economy: How to Lead in the New Age of Sectors without Borders* (Hoboken, NJ: John Wiley & Sons, 2023).

9   Danah Zohar, *Zero Distance: Management in the Quantum Age* (New York: Palgrave Macmillan, 2021), 66–67.

10 Chip Cutter, "CEO's Plan to Fix Bayer: Lose the Bosses," *Wall Street Journal*, March 23, 2024.

11 Pim de Morree, "Bayer's Bold Bet: How a 160-Year-Old Giant Is Liberating 100,000 People," November 17, 2024, www.Corporate-Rebels.com.

12 Bent Flyvbjerg, "Make Megaprojects More Modular," *Harvard Business Review*, November–December 2021.

13 Bartley J. Madden, "Bet on Innovation, Not Environmental, Social, and Governance Metrics, to Lead the Net Zero Transition," *Systems Research and Behavioral Science* 40, no. 3 (2023): 417–428.

14 Ed Catmull, *Creativity, Inc.: Overcoming the Unseen Forces That Stand in the Way of True Inspiration* (New York: Random House, 2014), 64–65.

15 James G. March, "Exploration and Exploitation in Organizational Learning," *Organization Science* 2, no. 1 (1991): 71–87. For a critique of treating exploitation and exploration separately, see Qijun Zhou, Rob Dekkers, and Robert Chia, "Are James March's 'Exploration' and 'Exploitation' Separable? Revisiting the Dichotomy in the Context of Innovation Management," *Technological Forecasting & Social Change*, article 122592, 2023.

16 Cayton M. Christensen and Michael Overdorf, "Meeting the Challenge of Disruptive Change," *Harvard Business Review*, March–April 2000.

17 Michael L. Tushman and Charles A. O'Reilly III, *Winning through Innovation: A Practical Guide to Leading Organizational Change and Renewal* (Boston: Harvard Business School Press, 2002), ix.

18 See Bartley J. Madden, *Value Creation Principles: The Pragmatic Theory of the Firm Begins with Purpose and Ends with Sustainable Capitalism* (Hoboken, NJ: John Wiley & Sons, 2020), 93–96, for a life-cycle analysis of Amazon.

19 Douglas E. Stevens, *Social Norms and the Theory of the Firm: A Foundational Approach* (Cambridge: Cambridge University Press, 2018).

20 John Seddon, *Freedom from Command and Control: A Better Way to Make the Work Work* (Buckingham, UK: Vanguard Education, Ltd., 2003), 153–154.

21 Nicolai J. Foss and Peter G. Klein, "Rethinking Hierarchy," *MIT Sloan Management Review,* spring, 56–61. See also Nicolai J. Foss and Peter G. Klein, *Why Managers Matter: The Perils of the Bossless Company* (New York: Public Affairs, 2023).

Chapter 5

1 Edward D. Hess, *Learn or Die: Using Science to Build a Leading-Edge Learning Organization* (New York: Columbia University Press, 2014), 75.

2 Bartley J. Madden, *My Value Creation Journey: An Autobiography of My Work* (Naples, FL: Bartley J. Madden Foundation, 2024).

3 Bartley J. Madden, *CFROI Valuation: A Total System Approach to Valuing the Firm* (Oxford: Butterworth-Heinemann, 1999), chapter 4.

4 Bartley J. Madden and Donn DeMuro, "Translator Simulation Software: Bridging the Gap between Accounting Returns and Economic Returns," *Journal of Applied Corporate Finance* Summer 2025; Bartley J. Madden, *Value Creation Principles: The Pragmatic Theory of the Firm Begins with Purpose and Ends with Sustainable Capitalism* (Hoboken, NJ: John Wiley & Sons, 2020); David A. Holland and Bryant A. Matthews, *Beyond Earnings: Applying the HOLT CFROI and Economic Profit Framework* (Hoboken, NJ: John Wiley & Sons, 2018).

5 Jacob Wolinsky, "My Interview with Stephen Penman: Professor of Accounting at the Columbia Business School," ValueWalk.com, August 10, 2011.

6 For a highly recommended technical discussion of the market-implied discount rate approach used by HOLT, see David A. Holand and

Bryant A. Matthews, *Beyond Earnings: Applying the HOLT CFROI and Economic Profit Framework* (Hoboken, NJ: John Wiley & Sons, 2018), chapter 7.

7   E. F. Fama and K. R. French, "Forecasting Profitability and Earnings," *Journal of Business* 73, no. 2 (2000): 161–175; Robert R. Wiggins and Timothy W. Ruefli, "Sustained Competitive Advantage: Temporal Dynamics and the Incidence and Persistence of Superior Economic Performance," *Organization Science* 13, no. 1 (2002): 82–105; Robert R. Wiggins and Timothy W. Ruefli, "Schumpeter's Ghost: Is Hyper-Competition Making the Best of Times Shorter?" *Strategic Management Journal* 26, no. 10 (2005): 887–911.

Chapter 6

1   Eric Hoffer, *Reflections on the Human Condition* (New York: Harper & Row Publishers, 1973), 22.

2   Financial Accounting Standards Board, Statement of Financial Accounting Concepts No. 8, OB2 and Concepts no. 8, BC1.5-BC1.6, Financial Accounting Foundation, as amended, December, 2021.

3   Shyam Sunder, "Rethinking Financial Reporting: Standards, Norms and Institutions," *Foundations and Trends in Accounting* 11, no. 1–2 (2016): 1–118.

4   Important research includes Baruch Lev, Bharat Sarah, and Theodore Sougiannis, "R&D Reporting Biases and Their Consequences," *Contemporary Accounting Research* 22, no. 4 (2005): 977–1026; Massimilano Bonacchi, Kalin Kolev, and Baruch Lev, "Customer Franchise—A Hidden, Yet Crucial Asset," *Contemporary Accounting Research* 32, no. 3 (2013): 1024–1049; and Luminita Enache and Anup Srivastava, "Should Intangible Investments Be Reported Separately or Commingled with Operating Expenses? New Evidence," *Management Science* 64, no. 7 (2018): 3446–3468.

5   Paul M. Romer, "Why, Indeed, in America? Theory, History, and the Origins of Modern Economic Growth," *American Economic Review* 86, no. 2 (1996): 202–206.

6   Mary E. Barth, Ken Li, and Charles G. McClure, "Evolution in Value Relevance of Accounting Information," *Accounting Review* 98, no. 1 (2023): 1–28, 1–2.

7   For example, Baruch Lev and Feng Gu, *The End of Accounting and the Path Forward for Investors and Managers* (Hoboken, NJ: John Wiley & Sons, 2016).

8   In my work, an after-tax, inflation-adjusted (real) 6 percent return has proven to be a useful long-term benchmark for the cost of capital. For historical data, see Bartley J. Madden, *CFROI Valuation: A Total System Approach to Valuing the Firm* (Oxford: Butterworth Heinemann, 1999).

9   For R&D intensive industries (e.g., biopharmaceutical), not only were there significant improvements in levels and trends of CFROIs, but also major improvements in reinvestment rates, which are critical for valuation analysis. Note that the simplicity of a single number for economic profit comes at a cost of not displaying reinvestment rates.

10 Baruch Lev, "Ending the Accounting-for-Intangibles Status Quo," *European Accounting Review* 28, no. 4 (2019): 713–736.

11 Aneel Iqbal, Shivaram Rajgopal, Anup Srivastava, and Rong Zhao, "Value of Internally Generated Intangible Capital," *Management Science*, forthcoming.

12 Bartley J. Madden and Donn DeMuro, "Translator Simulation Software: Bridging the Gap between Accounting Returns and Economic Returns," *Journal of Applied Corporate Finance*, forthcoming 2025.

13 G. C. Harcourt, "The Accountant in a Golden Age," *Oxford Economic Papers* 17, no. 1 (1965): 66–80, 80.

14 Franklin M. Fisher and John J. McGowan, "On the Misuse of Accounting Rates of Return to Infer Monopoly Profits," *American Economic Review* 73, no. 1 (1983): 82–97, 90.

15 Richard P. Brief, ed., *Estimating the Economic Rate of Return from Accounting Data* (New York: Garland Publishing, 1986).

16 Thomas R. Stauffer, "The Measurement of Corporate Rates of Return: A Generalized Formulation," *Bell Journal of Economics and Management Science* 2, no. 2 (1971): 434–469.

17 Yuji Ijiri, "Convergence of Cash Recovery Rate," in *Quantitative Planning and Control*, eds. Yuji Ijiri and Andrew B. Whinston (Cambridge, MA: Academic Press, 1979), 260–262, 20.

18 Andrew W. Stark, ed., *The Cash Recovery Approach to the Estimation of Economic Performance* (New York: Garland Publishing, 1990).

19 William R. Baber and Sok-Hyon Kang, "Estimates of Economic Rates of Return for the U.S. Pharmaceutical Industry, 1976–1987," *Journal of Accounting and Public Policy* 15, no. 4 (1996): 327–346.

20 Shivaram Rajgopal, Anup Srivastva, and Rong Zhao, "Do Digital Technology Firms Earn Excess Profits? Alternative Perspectives," *Accounting Review* 98, no. 4 (2023): 1–15, 4.

21 For different conceptual ways of handling R&D outlays and the resulting accounting data, see Healy, Myers, and Howe (2002) and Lev, Sarath, and Sougiannis (2005).

22 Bartley J. Madden and Donn DeMuro, "Translator Simulation Software: Bridging the Gap between Accounting Returns and Economic Returns," *Journal of Applied Corporate Finance*, forthcoming 2025.

23 Accounting lives for CapEx and intangibles were set to six years, and net working capital was 10 percent of total assets. For simplicity, equal cash receipts over the investment life were used, although the Translator can accommodate any pattern of cash receipts over the life of the investment.

Chapter 7

1 Richard A. Epstein, *Overdose: How Excessive Government Regulation Stifles Pharmaceutical Innovation* (New Haven: Yale University Press, 2006), 129.

2 Geoff Lawrence, "Focus at the FDA: Allowing the Market to Determine Effectiveness Could Lead to Better Health Outcomes While Ensuring the Food and Drug Administration Precludes the Distribution of Unsafe Products," Reason Foundation, August 2022.

3 Elazer R. Edelman, "Fear of Risk Threatens Medical Innovation," quoted in Jeremy Hsu, *InnovationNewsDaily*, June 29, 2011.

4   John Freund, MD, letter to the editor, *Wall Street Journal*, August 10, 2011, p. A14.

5   Sm Kazman, "Deadly Overcaution: FDA's Drug Approval Process," *Journal of Regulation and Social Costs* 1, no. 1 (1990): 41.

6   Mary J. Ruwart, *Death by Regulation: How We Were Robbed of a Golden Age of Health and How We Can Reclaim It* (Kalmazoo, MI: SunStar Press, 2018), 140–146.

7   Bartley J. Madden, "A Dual Track System to Give More-Rapid Access to New Drugs: Applying a Systems Mindset to the US Food and Drug Administration (FDA)," *Medical Hypotheses* 72, no. 2 (2009): 116–120.

8   Gregory Conko and Bartley J. Madden, "Free to Choose Medicine," *Administrative Law & Regulation* 14, no. 3 (2013): 4–13.

9   Edward Hudgins, "Free to Choose Medicine in Japan: A Model for America," *Heartland Institute Policy Brief*, 2018.

10 Douglas Sipp and Margaret Sleeboom-Faulkner, "Downgrading of Regulation in Regenerative Medicine," *Science* 365, no. 6454 (August 16, 2019): 644–646. For my reply, see Bartley J. Madden, "Science on FDA Liberalization: A Response to the Status Quo Process for Medical Treatments," *Econ Journal Watch* 17, no. 1 (2020): 90–97.

11 Jonathan J. Darrow, Ameet Sarpatwari, Jerry Avorn, and Aaron S. Kesselheim, "Practical, Legal, and Ethical Issues in Expanded Access to Investigational Drugs," *New England Journal of Medicine* 372, no. 3 (2015): 279–286.

12 Bartley J. Madden, *Free to Choose Medicine: Better Drugs Sooner at Lower Cost*, 3rd ed., (Arlington Heights, IL: Heartland Institute, 2018).

Chapter 8

1   Russell L. Ackoff, *Re-Creating the Corporation: A Design of Organizations for the 21st Century* (Oxford: Oxford University Press, 1999), 12.

2   See my website: www.LearningWhatWorks.com.

3   Publication milestones along my value creation journey include the following: Bartley J. Madden, "A Transactional Approach to Economic Research," *Journal of Socio-Economics* 20, no. 1 (1991):

57–71; Bartley J. Madden, "Management's Worldview: Four Critical Points about Reality, Language, and Knowledge Building to Improve Organizational Performance," *Journal of Organizational Computing and Electronic Commerce* 22, no. 4 (2012): 334–346; Bartley J. Madden, "Management's Key Responsibility," *Journal of Applied Corporate Finance* 30, no. 3 (2018): 27–35; Bartley J. Madden, *Value Creation Principles: The Pragmatic Theory of the Firm Begins with Purpose and Ends with Sustainable Capitalism* (Hoboken, NJ: John Wiley & Sons, 2020); Bartley J. Madden, "The Pragmatic Theory of the Firm," *Journal of Applied Corporate Finance* 33, no. 1 (2021): 98–110; Bartley J. Madden, "Understanding the Benefits of Capitalism through the Lens of a New Theory of the Firm," *Capitalism and Society* 17, no. 1 (2023): article 2; Bartley J. Madden and Douglas E. Stevens, "Extending the Pragmatic Theory of the Firm with Social Norms," *Journal of Applied Corporate Finance* Summer 2025.

4   Adam M. Brandenburger and Harborne W. Stuart Jr., "Value-Based Business Strategy," *Journal of Economics & Management Strategy* 5, no. 1 (1996): 5–24.

5   Joshua Gans and Michael D. Ryall, "Value Capture Theory: A Strategic Management Review," *Strategic Management Journal* 38, no. 1 (2017): 17–41.

6   Robert S. Kaplan and David P. Norton, "The Balanced Scorecard—Measures That Drive Performance," *Harvard Business Review*, January-February 1992.

7   Robert S. Kaplan and David P. Norton, *Strategy Maps: Converting Intangible Assets into Tangible Outcomes* (Boston, MA: Harvard Business School Press, 2004).

8   Bartley J. Madden, *Value Creation Principles: The Pragmatic Theory of the Firm Begins with Purpose and Ends with Sustainable Capitalism* (Hoboken, NJ: John Wiley & Sons, 2020).

9   Greg Milano, "Beyond EVA," *Journal of Applied Corporate Finance* 31, no. 3 (2019): 116–125.

10 Gary Hamel and Michele Zanini, *Humanocracy: Creating Organizations as Amazing as the People Inside Them* (Boston, MA: Harvard Business Review Press, 2020), 82–83.

11 Sumantra Ghoshal, "Bad Management Theories Are Destroying Good Management Practices," *Academy of Management Learning & Education* 4, no. 1 (2005): 75–91.

12 Werner H. Erhard, Michael C. Jensen, and Kari L. Granger, "Creating Leaders: An Ontological/Phenomenological Model," in *The Handbook for Teaching Leadership: Knowing, Doing, and Being*, eds. Scott Snook, Nitrin Nohria, and Rakesh Khurna (Thousand Oaks, CA: SAGE Publications, 2012). For insights about their model using the Knowledge-Building Loop, see Bartley J. Madden and Douglas E. Stevens, "Michael Jensen's Contributions to the Theory of the Firm: A Tribute in Three Acts," *Journal of Applied Corporate Finance* 36, no. 3 (2024): 117–125. My friend Werner Erhard has led a most unusual and productive life; for a deep dive into the philosophical foundation for his work, see Bruce Hyde and Drew Kopp, *Speaking Being: Werner Erhard, Martin Heidegger, and a New Possibility of Being Human* (Hoboken, NJ: John Wiley & Sons, 2019).